Following Freedom's Star

The Story of the
Underground Railroad

GREAT JOURNEYS

Following Freedom's Star

The Story of the Underground Railroad

by James Haskins
and
Kathleen Benson

BENCHMARK BOOKS

MARSHALL CAVENDISH
NEW YORK

*The authors are grateful to Katherine Butler Jones
and Brenda Parnes for their help.*

To Margaret Emily

Benchmark Books
Marshall Cavendish Corporation
99 White Plains Road
Tarrytown, NY 10591-9001

Cover photograph: *The Underground Railroad* by Charles T. Webber depicts a party of runaway slaves who managed to make their way to Indiana being welcomed by Levi and
Catherine Coffin, a Quaker couple active in the Underground Railroad.

Photo research by Candlepants Incorporated
Cover Photo: The Granger Collection
The photographs in this book are used by permission and through the courtesy of: *Archive
Photos*: 2–3, 54. *Corbis*: 20, 59, 70, 78,82, 86, 89, 90, 92; Bettmann Collection, 8, 14, 17;
Historical Picture Archive, 84. *The Philbrook Museum of Art, Tulsa Oklahoma, Gift of Laura
A. Clubb*: 19. *The Brooklyn Museum of Art, Gift of Gwendolyn O.L. Conkling*: 23. *Schomberg
Center for Research in Black Culture*: 26. *Gilbert Studios Washington DC*: 28. *North Carolina
State Archives*: 31, 33, 37. *Colonial Williamsburg Foundation/Designed and Drawn by Carl R.
Lounsbury*: 35. *The Granger Collection*: 40, 47, 52, 57, 61, 63, 67. *J. Winston Colman
Collection, Transylvania Library, Lexington, Kentucky*: 42, 74. *Oberlin College Archives*: 45.
New York Public Library Astor Lenox and Tilden Foundation: 48, 72. *His Promised Land, The
Autobiography of John P. Parker, Former Slave and Conductor on the Underground Railroad*: 49.
R.G. Dobard: 51 (left & right). *Madison County Historical Society, Onieda NY*: 65. *Ohio
Historical Society Archives and Library*: 76 (neg#11254), 81 (top) (neg. #ohs4371), 81
(low) (neg#ohs9373), 96 (neg#ohs10756). *Title page from Incidents in the Life of a Slave
Girl Written by Herself*, 95. *Mount Holyoke College Archive*: 98. *AP Wide World Photos*: Scott
Applewhite, 101; Wilton Historical Society/Douglas Healey,102; Steve Miller, 104.

Library of Congress Cataloging-in-Publication Data
Haskins, James, (date)
Following freedom's star: the story of the underground railroad / by James Haskins and
Kathleen Benson.
p. cm. — (Great journeys)
Includes bibliographical references and index.
ISBN 0-7614-1229-8
1. Underground railroad—Juvenile literature. 2. Fugitive slaves—United States—History—
19th century—Juvenile literature. [1. Underground railroad. 2. Fugitive slaves.] I. Benson,
Kathleen. II. Title. III. Great journeys (Benchmark Books (Firm))
E450 .H314   2001   973.7'115—dc21   2001025414

Printed in the United States of America

1 3 5 6 4 2

Contents

Also by James Haskins

Black, Grey, and Blue: African Americans in the Civil War

The Harlem Renaissance

Get on Board: The Story of the Underground Railroad

One More River to Cross: The Story of Twelve Black Americans

Outward Dreams: Black Inventors and Their Inventions

I Have a Dream: The Life and Words of Martin Luther King, Jr.

Black Dance in America: A History Through Its People

Power to the People: The Rise and Fall of the Black Panther Party

Separate, but Not Equal: The Dream and the Struggle

Also by James Haskins
and Kathleen Benson

African Beginnings

Bound for America: The Forced Migration of Africans to the New World

Out of the Darkness: The Story of Blacks Moving North, 1890–1940

Foreword

HARRIET ANN JACOBS WAS BORN AROUND 1813 IN THE TOWN OF Edenton, North Carolina. In her first years, she was raised in more fortunate circumstances than most other slave children. Her grandmother had been freed when she was middle aged, owned a house, and made her living as a baker. Her father was a slave, but he was such a skilled carpenter that in exchange for a payment of $200 per year, he was allowed to pursue his own clients and to manage his own affairs. He and his wife, also a slave, lived together in their own house and planned to raise their children there. Harriet later wrote, "I was so fondly shielded that I never dreamed I was a piece of merchandise, trusted to them for safe keeping, and liable to be demanded of them at any moment." [1]

Harriet's innocence came to an abrupt end when she was six years old. Her mother took ill and died. Only then did she realize that she was

Most slave children were put to work when they reached the age of six. That is the age at which Harriet Jacobs learned that she was a slave.

not legally a human being. As she wrote, "then, for the first time, I learned, by the talk around me, that I was a slave."[2] Harriet was taken to live in the home of her mistress, Margaret Horniblow, who taught her to read and to sew. Margaret Horniblow died when Harriet was eleven and willed young Harriet to her three-year-old niece, Mary Matilda Norcom. Harriet then went to live in the Norcom household.

Harriet became a house servant and thus did not have to do the backbreaking work of a field hand. But as she matured, she attracted the unwanted sexual attentions of her young owner's father, Dr. James Norcom. Miserable, she turned to a young white male neighbor, who offered to protect her. She bore two children by this man, Samuel Tredwell Taylor. But all the while, Dr. Norcom would not leave her alone. He used her children to try to persuade her to accept his attentions. When he threatened to sell her children if she did not relent, Harriet decided to escape. It was the only way she felt she could protect her young ones. Eventually, she made her way to New York City. Even in a free state, however, she was constantly in danger of being captured by slave catchers and returned to slavery in the South.

John P. Parker was born in Norfolk, Virginia, in 1827. He never knew his father, only that he was a white man and "one of the aristocrats of Virginia."[3] His mother was a slave, and thus all the children she bore were slaves as well. When Parker was eight years old, he was chained to an old male slave, walked to the capital city of Richmond, and sold to a local family. Not long afterward, he was sold again, this time to a slave trader. Chained to a group of other slaves—men, women, and children— he was marched deep into the South and sold in Alabama. It was June when the coffle, or file of slaves bound together, started on their journey. The mountains of Virginia were in bloom. "Every thing seemed to be gay except myself," Parker later recalled. He picked up a stick and began to strike at each flowering shrub. "That was my only revenge on things that were free."[4]

Treated so harshly at such a young age, Parker was unable to contain his hatred of slavery. Although his owner, a doctor, was kind to him, Parker was obstinate and acquired a reputation as being difficult. He started frequent fights, and after he tried and failed to escape, his owner decided to sell him. Parker persuaded a widow who was one of the doctor's patients to buy him, promising to pay her back. She did, and in this way, he purchased his own freedom. He moved first to Indiana and then to Ohio. In Cincinnati, he boarded with a black barber, who asked him to help rescue two slave girls in Maysville, Kentucky. Parker consented. He found the experience so exciting and satisfying that he became a "conductor" on the Underground Railroad. By his own account, over the course of fifteen years, he assisted more than four hundred slaves to find their way to freedom.

Harriet Jacobs and John Parker were only two of thousands of slaves who had both the courage to escape slavery and the good fortune to be aided by people who sympathized with their plight. Jacobs, in particular, could not have made a successful escape without the aid of countless others—black and white, slave and free. Once she left Edenton, she was helped by a group of people who believed that slavery was evil and that it was their responsibility to help free the enslaved. They worked together to assist runaways in escaping from bondage in the South to freedom in the North. Parker left for the North as a freeman, but once there he became one of many former slaves who were active in the loosely organized network known as the Underground Railroad.

By coincidence, both Jacobs and Parker were owned by doctors or doctors' families. Both were light complected. Both learned to read as slaves, which was an unusual circumstance. In most slave states it was against the law to educate slaves. Even more incredible, both went on to record their own stories. Jacobs wrote a book entitled *Incidents in the Life of a Slave Girl: Written by Herself* under the pen name Linda Brent. Parker told his story to an Ohio journalist. The manuscript, entitled *The*

Autobiography of John P. Parker, was finally issued in 1996, long after Parker's death. Although two individuals cannot possibly represent tens of thousands of people, through the lens of their unique experiences—and through their personal recollections—the story of the Underground Railroad comes to life.

THE UNDERGROUND RAILROAD WAS NEITHER UNDERGROUND NOR, IN most cases, a railroad. It was, however, secret and sometimes swift. It was perhaps the most clever and unique protest activity against slavery in the United States. It got its name from the actual railroads that were introduced to this country in 1830. The *Tom Thumb*, a steam-powered locomotive built by a New York merchant named Peter Cooper, had its first successful run that year. The change from horse-drawn engines to steam-powered ones began the great age of the railroad. For the first time in history, human beings could move quickly from one place to another. Naturally, the railroad gripped the imaginations of people who did not have that luxury.

Until recently, the term *Underground Railroad* was thought to have been coined around 1831—just one year after the first steam engine successfully reached its destination—by a hapless Kentucky slave owner. His slave, Tice Davids, had made a bold escape to freedom. With his master in hot pursuit, the story goes, Davids made his way to the Ohio River, which formed the border between the slave state of Kentucky and the free state of Ohio. In full view of his master, he plunged into the river and began to swim across. His master quickly found a boat and rowed out into the river, keeping Davids in view. But when Davids reached the opposite shore near the town of Ripley, Ohio, he vanished. Although his determined owner searched the countryside, he never found the fugitive. He finally concluded that the only way Davids could have escaped so quickly was by means of an "underground railroad."

The story may be a myth. Another legend traces the first use of the

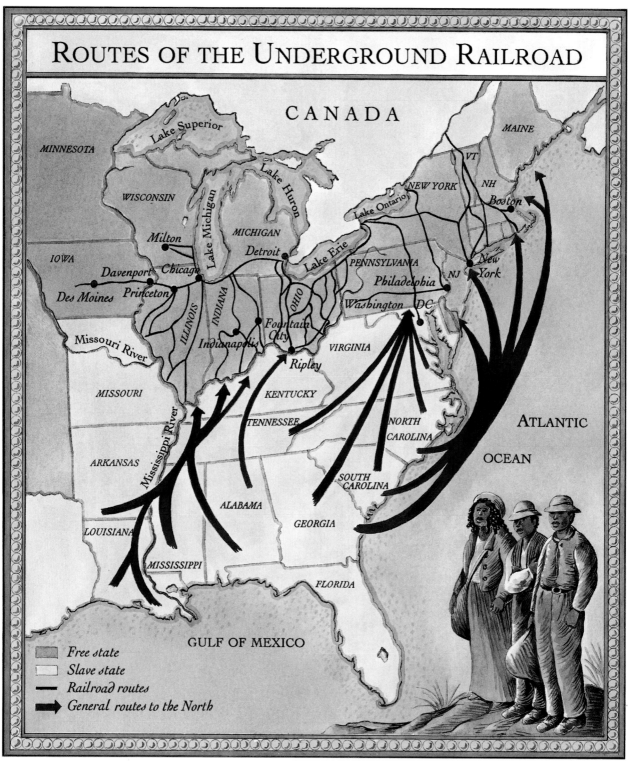

ROUTES OF THE UNDERGROUND RAILROAD

CANADA

MINNESOTA

Lake Superior

WISCONSIN

Lake Huron

MAINE

VT

NEW YORK

NH

Boston

IOWA

Milton

Lake Michigan

MICHIGAN

Detroit

Lake Erie

Lake Ontario

PENNSYLVANIA

New York

NJ

Davenport

Chicago

Des Moines

Princeton

ILLINOIS

INDIANA

OHIO

Philadelphia

Washington

DC

Missouri River

Indianapolis

Fountain City

Ripley

VIRGINIA

MISSOURI

KENTUCKY

ATLANTIC

TENNESSEE

NORTH CAROLINA

OCEAN

ARKANSAS

Mississippi River

SOUTH CAROLINA

ALABAMA

GEORGIA

LOUISIANA

MISSISSIPPI

FLORIDA

GULF OF MEXICO

- Free state
- Slave state
- Railroad routes
- General routes to the North

The routes were many, but the goal was the same—to live in freedom. Several towns and cities in the North became key "stations" along the way.

term to Chester County, Pennsylvania. John P. Parker supported Ripley, Ohio's, claim to be the place where the term originated. But the incident he related dates the origin of the term to just after the War of 1812. Citing the statement of "an old citizen who claimed to be present at the time of the incident," Parker said: "It was in the upper shipyard on Red Oak Creek. . . . The fugitive ran amongst the piles of lumber and disappeared. One of the workmen, when asked by the master if he had seen the fugitive, answered, 'The slave disappeared so quickly he must have gone on an underground road.' The term 'rail' was fixed after the introduction of steam [rail]roads."[5] However it got started, the term stuck, for it combined the freedom of movement the railroad offered with the mystery of a secret network.

Networks of assistance to fugitive slaves had existed since colonial times. They did not become a major force until the advent of the organized abolition movement in the nineteenth century. This movement, fueled by those who called for an immediate end to the practice, gained strength in the 1830s. By 1840, there were some five hundred abolitionist organizations in the United States. As the movement grew, so did the activity of the Underground Railroad, which peaked between 1830 and 1865. With the end of the Civil War, slavery was abolished in the United States and the Underground Railroad ended its run. Historians estimate that between 75,000 and 100,000 fugitive slaves were transported to freedom via the Underground Railroad. Although there is really no way to know the complete story of an activity that was conducted in such secrecy, by the 1990s great strides were being taken to identify and preserve Underground Railroad sites and to chronicle the lives of the people who worked and traveled on that unique path to freedom.

Crispus Attucks, an escaped slave, was the first American to die in the Boston Massacre, the riot that led to the outbreak of the Revolutionary War.

One

The Will to Be Free

HARRIET JACOBS WROTE, "EVERY WHERE THE YEARS BRING TO ALL enough of sin and sorrow; but in slavery the very dawn of life is darkened by these shadows." [1] John Parker said of his time in bondage, "It was not the physical part of slavery that made it cruel and degrading, it was the taking away from a human being the initiative, of thinking, of doing his own ways." [2] From the beginning of slavery in North America, men and women in bondage fought against their captivity. They revolted, they committed suicide, and they ran away. Running away was obviously the most common method of seeking freedom. The first American to die in the cause of the American Revolution was a fugitive slave. Crispus Attucks was killed by a British soldier's musket ball in the Boston Massacre in 1770. Attucks's story is lost in the mists of history, but it is likely that he had some help, either during or after his escape.

The first abolition society was formed in Philadelphia in 1775. Its aim was to intervene in cases in which blacks and Indians claimed to have been illegally enslaved. Nothing in its statement of purpose mentioned aiding fugitives. However, the founders of the society were Quakers, and they believed it was their God-given duty to help human beings be free.

Formally known as the Religious Society of Friends, the Quakers were founded in England in the middle of the seventeenth century. Their critics nicknamed them Quakers because their founder, George Fox, told them to "tremble at the word of the Lord." Persecuted in England, many traveled to the New World seeking religious freedom. The colony of Pennsylvania was established by William Penn as a haven for his fellow Quakers. Its original constitution guaranteed freedom for slaves. The first antislavery pamphlet published in the colonies was written in 1693 by a Quaker named George Keith. Not all Quakers were against slavery. Some owned slaves; others refused to work against slavery. In fact, by 1700 slavery was recognized as a legal institution in Pennsylvania. But enough Pennsylvania Quakers were against slavery to form an organization dedicated to its abolition.

After the Revolutionary War ended, the thirteen colonies sent representatives to a series of conventions in order to draft a constitution that would officially unite the former colonies into a group of united states. The process was not always smooth. Many issues divided the states and had to be resolved before they would all agree to live under one set of federal laws. Slavery was a major issue. Most northern states were against it, while most southern states supported it. The delegates to the constitutional conventions compromised. The Ordinance of 1787 forbade slavery north of the Ohio River. It also established the Virginia Military District of Ohio, to be settled by Virginia planters who wished to free their slaves. Two large free settlements were established in the district, to which southern planters could send their slaves to be freed. Thus, antislavery men were attracted to the district. When Ohio joined the Union in 1803, it was admitted as a free state—separated by the Ohio River

William Penn established the colony of Pennsylvania with a constitution that guaranteed freedom for former slaves.

from the slave state of Virginia and the slave territory of Kentucky.

Another problem that concerned the framers of the new government was that of fugitive slaves. Southern slaveholders were rightly worried that their slaves would escape to free states. They wanted a clause in the new U.S. Constitution that forbade helping fugitives. Many northern delegates were against such a clause. They were also against using the terms *slave* and *slavery* in this document of freedom. Eventually, a poor compromise was reached. The offending terms appear nowhere in the Constitution. But a clause concerning fugitives, or runaways, clearly includes them. Introduced at the Philadelphia Constitutional Convention of 1787, the clause refers to persons "held in service or labor." It was included as a response to the fact that fugitives from slave states were being aided by people in other states.

Two years later, the new nation elected its first government. As the representatives of the various states tried to work together, the issue of fugitive slaves kept coming up. Many free states refused to assist slave owners in regaining their lost property, and the supporters of slavery decided that a law was needed that specifically addressed the problem. In 1793, Congress passed a Fugitive Slave Act, which made it a crime to help an escaped slave.

None other than the first president of the United States tried to avail himself of that law after one of his slaves escaped. The slave was Ona Judge. She was probably born in 1774 at Mount Vernon, George Washington's Virginia plantation. Her father, Andrew Judge, was a white indentured servant from Leeds, England. Her mother was a slave named Betty who belonged to Martha Custis Washington. George Washington was Martha's second husband. Her property, consisting of both land and slaves, became his.

After Washington was elected the new nation's first president in 1789, he and his wife moved to New York City, which served briefly as the capital of the United States. Ona was among the seven slaves they took with them. She accompanied the Washingtons to Philadelphia a year and a half later, after the seat of government was moved there. As the president's term in office drew to a close, and the Washingtons began to make plans to return to Mount Vernon, Ona realized that if she were to return to the South, she might never be free.

"I had friends among the colored people of Philadelphia," she recalled years later, "had my things carried there before hand, and left while [the Washingtons] were eating dinner." [3] After she was safely hidden, her friends walked the docks looking for a northbound ship whose captain would not ask questions. Ona found passage on the sloop *Nancy*,

The United States was just a few years old when congressmen from slave states succeeded in passing the first Fugitive Slave Act in 1793.

President George Washington cited the terms of the Fugitive Slave Act to justify his attempt to reclaim his runaway slave, Ona Judge.

captained by John Bowles of Portsmouth, New Hampshire. In Portsmouth, Ona had the great misfortune to be recognized by the daughter of New Hampshire senator John Langdon, who knew Martha Washington. This sighting by Betsy Langdon is probably how Washington learned the whereabouts of his slave. Washington wrote to Portsmouth authorities asking their help. In a letter dated September 1, 1796, he requested that the city's collector of customs "seize her and put her on board a Vessel bound immediately to this place, or to Alexandria." [4] The officer, one William Whipple, was set to comply with the former president's wishes. When he interviewed Ona Judge, however, he was struck by her earnest desire for freedom. He wrote to the president that he could not force her back into slavery because "popular opinion here is in favor of universal freedom." [5]

It should be noted that New Hampshire had a very small black population. Most were free. The few slaves worked as servants to the wealthy. In general, the citizens of New Hampshire were against slavery. Thus, it was possible for a federal officer—collector of customs—to defy not only the Fugitive Slave Act of 1793 but also the president of the United States and get away with it.

While Washington continued to entreat Whipple to help, Ona Judge found lodging with a free black family in Portsmouth and worked as a seamstress. In January 1797 she met and married Jack Staines, a free black seaman, and later gave birth to a daughter. Nevertheless, she was in constant fear of recapture. Two years after Ona Staines settled in Portsmouth, Washington learned that a nephew was planning a business trip to New Hampshire. He asked him to try and seize the woman, along with any children she might have. But Senator John Langdon heard of the plan and got word to Ona. Fearful for her safety and unable to seek help from her husband, who was at sea, Staines escaped with her baby in a wagon to Greenland, New Hampshire. She hid in the home of a free black family named Jacks and remained there until Washington's nephew left New Hampshire and her husband returned from sea. Not until Washington's death three months later did she feel completely safe.

The Staines had two more children, a son and a daughter, and maintained their own household in Portsmouth. After her husband's death in 1803, Ona Staines took a job as a live-in maid with a local family. Soon after, however, she moved to Greenland to live with the people who had sheltered her before. Her son, William, left home in the 1820s to become a sailor and never returned from sea. Her two daughters, Eliza and Nancy, worked as servants in the homes of neighbors. Both died before their mother. Alone and in poverty for the last fifteen years of her life, Ona Judge Staines depended on the people of Greenland for donations of firewood and food. Although she admitted that her life would have been easier if she had remained with the Washingtons at Mount Vernon, she never regretted leaving them. When asked if she did, she replied, "No, I am free, and have, I trust, been made a child of God by the means." She died on February 25, 1848. [6]

ALTHOUGH FUGITIVE SLAVES could feel fairly safe once they reached the northern free states, there was always the chance that local authorities or proslavery citizens would seize them and return them to bondage. Thus, after the War of 1812, Canada became the favored destination of most slaves. If they could make it to Canada, they were beyond the reach of U.S. law.

Slavery had existed in Canada with the arrival of the first French settlers. It was legalized in French-held Canada, which was called New France, in 1705. In 1763, after the end of the Seven Years' War, New France came under British control. Slavery continued to exist. A dozen years later, the American colonies declared their independence from Great Britain. During the war that followed, the British tried to bolster

Eastman Johnson was inspired by daring slave escapes to paint A Ride for Liberty: The Fugitive Slaves *in 1862.*

their sagging armies by offering freedom to enslaved American blacks in exchange for military service. Even though they lost the war, the British kept their promise. In 1783, the same year as Great Britain signed the Paris Peace Treaty granting the thirteen former colonies their independence, some 5,000 blacks from the United States crossed the border into Canada. Most of them settled in the Maritime Provinces—Nova Scotia, New Brunswick, and Prince Edward Island. Of them, about one-third were former slaves. From then on, Canada was regarded as a safe haven for those escaping the shackles of slavery.

During the War of 1812, which began when U.S. forces invaded Canada, the British again offered freedom and this time land to escaped slaves. Thousands of black volunteers fought for Great Britain. Seeking refuge behind British lines, in 1813 nearly 2,000 escaped slaves made their way to Nova Scotia. Overwhelmed by this influx, Nova Scotia banned further black immigration two years later. But the province then called Upper Canada encouraged black immigration to the sparsely populated area, so passage to the north continued unchecked. The slave and abolitionist grapevines spread the word that Canada was the place to go. John P. Parker says in his autobiography that "after the War of 1812 every slave knew the north star led to freedom and Canada. From 1812 the gauntlet of war was thrown down between the friends and enemies of the fugitive, and [there was] incessant warfare. . . . "[7]

Canada could have signed an agreement with the United States in which it pledged to return all fugitive slaves. Such extradition agreements are often signed when a U.S. citizen accused of a crime flees to another country to avoid prosecution and that nation agrees to return, or extradite, the fugitive. But Canadian authorities refused to comply. In fact, in 1841, the British crown formally announced that fugitive slaves would be free in Canada.

A history of Tazewell County, Illinois, published in 1879, states it this way:

From mere goods and chatels in our liberty-boasting nation they were transformed into men and women; from being hunted with side-arms and blood-hounds, like wild beasts, they were recognized and respected as good and loyal subjects by the Queen as soon as their feet touched British soil. . . . In February, 1841, there came a day of jubilee to the doubting ones, when Queen Victoria's proclamation was read to them: "That every fugitive from United States slavery be recognized and protected as a British subject the moment his or her foot touched the soil of her domain." [8]

Religious songs sung by American slaves, called spirituals, had long included references to Canaan, also known as the Promised Land to the Jews. Before slavery was abolished in Canada, Canaan was often used as a code word for the North. Frederick Douglass was probably one of the most famous fugitive slaves. In his autobiography, he wrote that during their flight to freedom, he and his five companions frequently sang:

> O Canaan, sweet Canaan,
> I am bound for the land of Canaan.

It is probably no coincidence that the organized network of people dedicated to helping fugitive slaves reach freedom was born around the same time slavery was abolished in Canada. But there were many other reasons as well. One was the growth of the abolitionist movement. Some people had always believed that slavery was wrong. But it took other circumstances to spur them to form organizations pledged to fight it. Added to the determination of many Quakers to help their enslaved fellow human beings, a great religious revival swept the country in the early part of the century. It urged the faithful to end sinful practices, of which some believed slavery was the most evil. It presented a vision of human perfection, which abolitionists felt they could attain by helping to end slavery.

The New England Anti-Slavery Society was formed in 1832 by eleven whites. Two years later, the American Anti-Slavery Society was organized in Philadelphia. Three blacks were among its founders, and sixty-two blacks signed the society's Declaration of Sentiments. Whites were more numerous, more influential, and more free to move about. But rather than replacing the looser network of blacks—slave and free—and whites who had been helping fugitive slaves from the beginning, those who were active in the Underground Railroad established a network that in many ways was parallel to it.

Organizations such as the Philadelphia Vigilance Committee were formed by blacks and whites to assist fugitive slaves in their flight to freedom.

The only known photograph of Harriet Jacobs, taken in 1894 when she was about eighty years old.

Two

Harriet Jacobs Escapes

When Harriet Jacobs decided to escape in 1835, she was helped by her own friends and relatives. In the small town of Edenton, North Carolina, and the surrounding area, news traveled fast and everyone knew everyone else's business. It was no secret that Dr. James Norcom, the father of Jacobs's young owner, was using his power over her two young children—six-year-old Joseph and three-year-old Louisa Matilda—to pressure her to become his mistress.

The fact that the father of Jacobs's two children was a white neighbor of the Norcoms did not diminish Dr. Norcom's desire for Harriet. He offered to give her a house where she could raise her children. When she refused, he sent her to Auburn, one of his plantations, located twelve miles out of town. Jacobs went, hoping that her children would be left in the care of her grandmother.

The Norcoms's son, William Jr., married shortly afterward and took his bride to live at Auburn. Dr. Norcom arranged for both Harriet Jacobs and her brother John to serve the young couple. When Jacobs learned that Dr. Norcom also planned to send the children to Auburn to be "broken in" as plantation slaves, she was determined to spare them the harshness of such a life. She believed that if she were gone, none of the Norcoms would want to be bothered with raising two young slave children and would be more likely to sell them to their father or great-grandmother.

One night in June 1835, twenty-one-year-old Harriet Jacobs stole away from the plantation and returned to Edenton. There, she spent the night hiding in the home of a black friend. That same night, a woman boarder in her grandmother's house quietly packed all of Jacobs's belongings and hid them to make it look as if Jacobs had taken her possessions with her.

Before the next day was over, a reward poster for her capture was circulating:

$300 REWARD! Ran away from the subscriber, an intelligent, bright, mulatto girl, named Harriet, 21 years of age. Five feet four inches high. Dark eyes, and black hair inclined to curl; but it can be made straight. Has a decayed spot on a front tooth. She can read and write, and in all probability will try to get to the Free States. All persons are forbidden, under penalty of the law, to harbor or employ said slave. $150 will be given to whoever takes her in the state, and $300 if taken out of the state and delivered to me, or lodged in jail.

Dr. Norcom [1]

In addition to posted flyers, Dr. Norcom placed advertisements in eight issues of the *American Beacon*, a daily newspaper published in Norfolk, Virginia. In these ads, he offered only a one hundred dollar reward. It was common for slave owners to offer a large reward immediately after

Dr. James Norcom placed this advertisement calling for the capture of Harriet Jacobs in a Norfolk, Virginia, newspaper.

$100 REWARD

WILL be given for the apprehension and delivery of my Servant Girl HARRIET. She is a light mulatto, 21 years of age, about 5 feet 4 inches high, of a thick and corpulent habit, having on her head a thick covering of black hair that curls naturally, but which can be easily combed straight. She speaks easily and fluently, and has an agreeable carriage and address. Being a good seamstress, she has been accustomed to dress well, has a variety of very fine clothes, made in the prevailing fashion, and will probably appear, if abroad, tricked out in gay and fashionable finery. As this girl absconded from the plantation of my son without any known cause or provocation, it is probable she designs to transport herself to the North.

The above reward, with all reasonable charges, will be given for apprehending her, or securing her in any prison or jail within the U. States.

All persons are hereby forewarned against harboring or entertaining her, or being in any way instrumental in her escape, under the most rigorous penalties of the law.

JAMES NORCOM.

Edenton, N. C. June 30

discovering the absence of a fugitive but to reduce it to a smaller amount once the first ads proved ineffective in securing the runaway's return. These ads described her further as "of a thick and corpulent habit," meaning she was fat. They also commented on her wardrobe: "Being a good seamstress, she has been accustomed to dress well, has a variety of very fine clothes, made in the prevailing fashion, and will probably appear, if abroad, tricked out in gay and fashionable finery." [2]

Dr. Norcom had no idea that Harriet Jacobs was still in Edenton. Like most other blacks who escaped from slavery and then either told or wrote down their story, Jacobs did not give details about her escape. She did not want to reveal the names of people who had helped her, for fear that they would be arrested or otherwise punished. She had hid at first in the home of a black woman neighbor. Then she was concealed in the home of a well-to-do white woman who held slaves herself but sympathized with Jacobs. Hiding out in a small storeroom above the woman's bedroom, Jacobs could actually look out a window and watch Dr. Norcom pass by on his way to and from his office. Only the woman and one trusted slave knew of Jacobs's whereabouts in the house. After a while, however, Jacobs feared that some of the woman's other slaves were getting suspicious. So one night in August 1835, Jacobs, dressed as a sailor, was led by a friend to Snaky Swamp, where she spent the night. It was the only night she experienced what many less fortunate fugitives, who did not have friends or family to help them, were forced to face. One wonders if she, like countless fugitives before and after her, trembled at the sounds of the swamp night and tried to find the North Star, hoping to see the beacon that could guide her to freedom. The next day, still dressed in sailor's clothing, she walked through the streets to her grandmother's house, where a hiding place had been prepared for her.

A small shed had been added to the house years before. Under the roof was a small garret, nine feet long and seven feet wide. Jacobs's uncle Mark had made and concealed a trapdoor. The peak of the garret was only three feet high. She could not sit upright. When she slept, she could not even turn over without hitting the roof. Her arms and legs grew stiff from the cramped conditions. There was no light and very little air. She eventually managed to bore a few holes in the wall so she could see out into the street. In that way, she could also see to read. She lived for the times when her children passed by and she could catch a glimpse of them. She never imagined that this cramped hiding place would be her home for nearly seven years.

Harriet Jacobs probably hid in one place longer than any other fugitive

A photograph of a man believed to be Dr. James Norcom.

slave in history. Her small garret refuge was one of the most uncomfortable a slave ever had to inhabit in the quest for freedom. But rarely were hiding places for fugitives comfortable.

While Jacobs hid in her garret, Dr. Norcom made several trips to New York and also questioned her children. But they had no idea their mother was living in their house. To keep him thinking that she had managed to make it to the North, Jacobs and her friends arranged for her to write a letter, which was then posted to him from Boston. The ruse was convincing, as Dr. Norcom began to search for her there and even wrote to the city's mayor for help.

As Jacobs had suspected, once she was gone Dr. Norcom had little

Hiding Places

A variety of small spaces served as hiding places for fugitive slaves. Several features of eighteenth-century houses could be adapted for the purpose. In that era, when all cooking and heating were done in open fireplaces, a lot of wood ash was created, which was a messy but necessary job to remove. Some houses had a channel from the rear of the fireplace to a holding bin. Ashes that accumulated in the fireplace were swept into this channel, from which they dropped to the holding bin, making it unnecessary to take the ashes out of the house more than once a season. By about 1825, when more efficient stoves became available, some fireplaces were bricked up. It is possible that some Underground Railroad station operators used the holding bins for hiding fugitives. The Elijah Lewis House in Farmington, Massachusetts, a confirmed Underground Railroad station, has a removable stone that gives access to the holding bin.

Cellar vaults used as root cellars or for winter food storage were also used as hiding places, as were small spaces under the garrets in attics. When bedchambers were constructed in attics, part of the attic was walled off, creating a crawl space accessible by means of a small door. This crawl space could easily hide a fugitive slave.

In the northern states, underground tunnels were sometimes built between the house and the barn so that the barn could be easily reached in winter. Houses located next to rivers sometimes were connected to the banks by means of a tunnel. The Vernon Lee House in Norwich, Massachusetts, has such a tunnel. So did the John Holyoke House in Brewer, Maine. That tunnel lay forgotten and unused for more than a century before it was discovered in 1995, when the house was torn down.

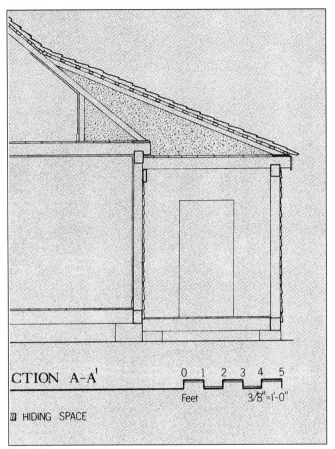

A scale drawing of the attic hiding place in which Harriet Jacobs spent nearly seven years. How long do you think you could last in such a cramped space?

CTION A-A¹

0 1 2 3 4 5

Feet   3/8"=1'-0"

HIDING SPACE

use for her children. He had only been interested in using them to manipulate her. Although his young daughter was their rightful owner, he allowed their father to buy them. Samuel Tredwell Sawyer let his children continue to live with their great-grandmother. He had told Jacobs that he would free the children, but failed to keep his word. In 1837, Sawyer ran for Congress and won the election, despite every effort by the Norcoms to help his opponent. He left Edenton for Washington, D.C., without freeing the children. He took Jacobs's brother, John, with him. The following year, he married Levinia Peyton in Chicago.

For their honeymoon, Sawyer took his bride to New York for a few days, then to Canada, before returning to Edenton. John Jacobs accompanied them. As soon as they reached Chicago, he had started to look for a way to escape, for he was now in the North. He went to the English customhouse and tried to secure a "seaman's protection," which were papers stating that he was a freeman and a sailor in service to England. John Jacobs could not bring himself to lie about who he really was, however, and could not get the necessary documents. In New York, he decided to pursue freedom in a different way. He arranged to sail to Providence, Rhode Island. After waiting on the Sawyers as they dined at the Hotel Astor, he slipped out. Unable to write, he had arranged for a friend to draft the following letter, which Sawyer received the following morning: "Sir—I have left you, not to return; when I have got settled, I will give you further satisfaction. No longer yours, John S. Jacobs." [3]

In 1840, the Sawyers summoned Harriet Jacobs's daughter, Louisa Matilda, to Washington to care for the couple's new baby. Jacobs hated the thought of her daughter tending her own freeborn half sister. Just before Louisa Matilda left Edenton, Jacobs arranged to spend a night with her daughter in the bedroom she had occupied in her grandmother's house. Her grandmother advised her not to take such a risk and also warned Jacobs of the added danger of trusting her young daughter with her secret. While her uncle Mark kept watch at the gate, Harriet and her seven-year-old daughter had a tearful reunion. Louisa promised not to tell her mother's secret, and she never did.

In June 1842, after nearly seven years, Harriet Jacobs left her garret for good. Just before she left, she spoke with her son for the first time since going into hiding and learned that he had suspected she was in the house all along. He had once heard a cough coming from the shed and believed it was hers.

Compared to many other fugitive slaves, Harriet Jacobs had an easy journey north. She was light complected, knew how to read and write, spoke in a cultured manner, wore clothing in the latest fashion she had sewn for herself, and had a network of friends and family who could

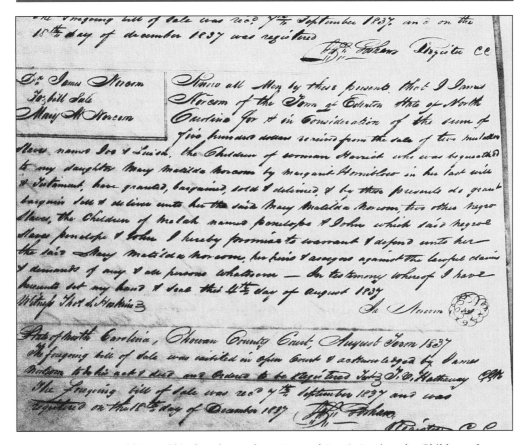

Dr. James Norcom sold two of his daughter's slaves "named Joe & Louisa, the Children of woman Harriet." This note indicates that he substituted Jacobs's children with two other young slaves and that the debt is paid in full.

provide her with money and connections. Also, she lived in a port city and could travel by water rather than overland. Arrangements had been made for Jacobs to travel on a ship whose captain charged an exorbitant fee. He was a southerner whose own brother had been a slave trader, but he felt that slavery was degrading to all connected with it. He escorted Jacobs to a little cabin aboard the ship that would take her to freedom. There, she was astonished to find her friend Hannah Pritchard, who was escaping as well.

Following Freedom's Star

Slaves used a variety of means to communicate. As in Africa, they used drumbeats—and even the rhythmic tapping of their feet while dancing—to send coded messages. Slaves also communicated by means of songs. Some religious hymns and spirituals came to have a double meaning when sung by slaves. For example, reference to Moses, the character in the Bible who led the Israelites out of slavery in Egypt, could also mean someone who helped slaves to escape.

One folk song actually contained directions for following the Underground Railroad. It was called "Follow the Drinking Gourd," and according to legend it was taught to slaves in the Deep South by a free black man who traveled about teaching slaves how to escape. This man, a one-legged sailor named Peg Leg Joe, would hire himself out as a plantation handyman. In 1859, his activities centered around Mobile, Alabama.[1] He would make friends with the slaves and teach them the song.

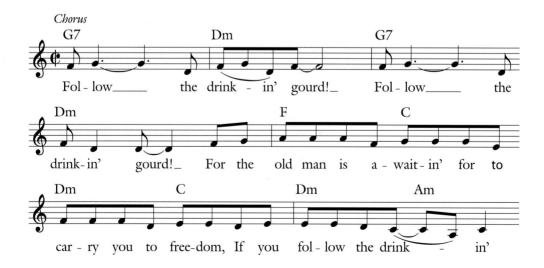

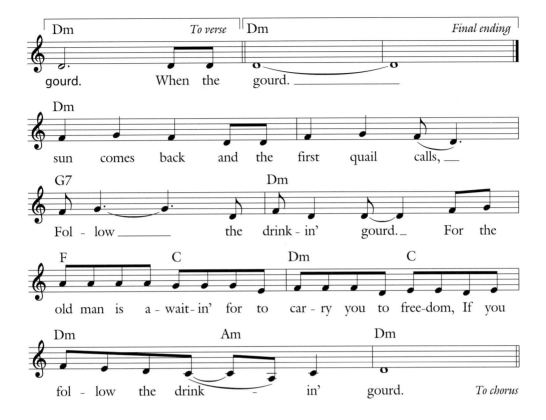

The riverbank will make a very good road,
The dead trees show you the way.
Left foot, peg foot, traveling on,
Follow the drinking gourd.

The river ends between two hills,
Follow the drinking gourd.
There's another river on the other side,
Follow the drinking gourd.

When the great big river meets the little river,
Follow the drinking gourd.
For the old man is a-waiting for to carry you to freedom
If you follow the drinking gourd.

The drinking gourd was a nickname for the Big Dipper, which points to the North Star. The references to the sun coming back and the quail call meant that slaves should travel in the springtime. The river that "ends between two hills" was the Tombigbee River in Mississippi. The second river was the Tennessee River, and the "great big river" was the Ohio River. The legend holds that after teaching the slaves the song, Peg Leg Joe would leave the plantation, promising to meet them at the "great big river." When they arrived, he would ferry them across to the free states on the other side, where they followed one of the Underground Railroad routes to Canada.

This drawing was made after the Civil War. When Harriet Jacobs sailed to the North, blacks aboard ships were not so numerous, or so calm and happy.

The captain explained to the women that if anyone asked, he would say they were traveling to join their husbands in Philadelphia, but no one was suspicious of them. Ten days after setting sail from Edenton, the ship arrived in Philadelphia. It was Jacobs's first time in a large city, and she was overwhelmed by the crowds and the bustle of activity. The captain spotted a respectable-looking black man and asked him to help the two women. The man turned out to be the Reverend Jeremiah Durham, a black minister who was active in the Philadelphia Vigilant Committee. This organization, whose membership was mostly black, had ties to the city's Anti-Slavery Society. Durham helped the two women find a ladies clothing shop, where Harriet bought gloves and double veils for both herself and her friend to hide their faces and hands from prying eyes. Durham also arranged lodging for them with black families in Philadelphia. "That night," wrote Harriet, "I sought my pillow with feelings I had never carried before. I verily believed myself to be a free woman."[4]

A rare photograph of an even rarer event—several generations of one slave family together. It was much more common for families to be broken up and sold, often never to see each other again.

Three

John P. Parker Escapes

THE FIRST TIME JOHN P. PARKER HAD A CHANCE TO ESCAPE FROM SLAVERY, he was in Philadelphia. Coincidentally, he was there around 1843, the year Harriet Jacobs and her friend Hannah Pritchard arrived by boat from North Carolina in their flight to the North. Far from being a fugitive, however, Parker was a body servant to the two young sons of his master. They were on their way to college at Yale University in New Haven, Connecticut, and the plan was for Parker to accompany them as their servant. He was looking forward to the opportunity to learn along with his young masters, for like Harriet Jacobs he was one of the rare southern slaves who had been taught to read and write.

Parker's life had improved somewhat since his childhood march to the Deep South as part of a slave coffle. He had escaped the fate of most of his fellow captives, who had been put to work either clearing fields for cotton planting or growing cotton. As he recalled years later, "Cotton was in demand, each field was a gold mine, so that Virginia, Kentucky, and Missouri, where cotton could not be raised, were the new breeding places for the slaves, who were sold south like their mules to clear away their forests. It was into this situation that the men and women of our caravan were hurled, while the boys and girls were sent on into towns until they were stronger." [1]

Parker was taken into Mobile, Alabama, where he was bought by a physician whom Parker later described as a gentleman and kind hearted. As well as he treated his young slave, however, the doctor was not the one to teach him to read and write. An Alabama law, strictly enforced, forbade the education of slaves. But that did not stop the doctor's young sons from sharing their lessons with their playmate and from smuggling books to him from the family library. If he was not driving the doctor around in a wagon to visit patients, Parker would sneak into the barn and read up in the hayloft. When it came time for the boys to go to Yale, Parker was delighted to learn that he would be going with them. The boys promised him all the books he could read, and he looked forward to getting an unofficial college education while his young masters got theirs. He was given a complete new outfit of clothes for the trip. He was sixteen years old and thrilled at the prospects for his future, considering that he was a slave.

Parker accompanied the doctor and the two boys as they traveled from Mobile to New Orleans by boat, up the Mississippi by steamboat, then on to Pittsburgh. From Pittsburgh, they went by carriage to Philadelphia—a hotbed of abolitionism, although Parker did not know that. He was standing outside the hotel where they were staying one evening, when a distinguished-looking gentleman approached him and whispered, "Look out tonight." That evening when Parker went to his room, he found a note on his pillow that read, "Be ready tonight." [2] Puzzled, he took the note to his master, who quickly understood that Philadelphia abolitionists were planning to liberate his slave. That was

Abolitionist groups assumed many forms, each with its own antislavery philosophy. This Oberlin, Ohio, group advocated action. They rescued slaves who were about to be returned to their masters.

the end of Parker's hopes to "attend college." Rather than going to New Haven, he returned with his owner to Mobile.

Parker was apprenticed to a plasterer, whose physical abuse sent Parker to the local slave hospital. While there, Parker saw the white woman who ran the hospital beating an ailing slave woman. He was so angry that he seized the whip and beat the offender. Aware that not even his influential owner could protect him, he decided to run away. He sneaked on board a steamer bound for New Orleans and on arrival hid out on the docks. Aching with hunger, he found his way to a large house, where a black cook pretended not to notice him. She stirred a large pot of soup steaming on the fire, laid out a bowl and spoon, and then left the kitchen. Parker ate his fill of soup, then returned to the docks and stowed away on another steamer. He was discovered and taken prisoner by the captain, who at the next stop placed him in the custody of the local sheriff. Sent out to work on a farm, Parker escaped, hid out in a swamp, and eventually stole onto one of three flatboats that were lashed together, carrying hogsheads of tobacco. He was soon found out by the boats' skippers, and their discovery put them in a quandary.

Parker was worth about $1,800, and, as he later explained the boatmen's position, "anyone who aided me was a thief, worse than a thief, an enemy to the institution of slavery. So the hand of the law, the anger of the people, and the consolidated fear of the south were all in hot cry after anyone who helped to break down their institutions. The penalties were severe—not only sending the rescuer to jail but confiscating his property as well." [3]

The three flatboat men who captured John Parker were no abolitionists. In fact, they decided to avoid trouble by simply murdering Parker, discussing their plan openly so he was certain he was breathing his last breaths. Fortunately for Parker, one of the men changed his mind and allowed him to escape again by running down a plank toward shore. Eventually, he made his way back to the New Orleans docks and was planning his next move when a hand touched his shoulder. "Well, well," said the voice of his owner, the doctor from Mobile. [4]

Parker was put to work learning the trade of an iron molder. But he continually displeased his bosses. Eventually, his owner decided to sell him, and Parker knew that meant the cotton fields of Alabama were in his future. He persuaded an elderly patient of the doctor's to buy him, promising in turn to purchase his freedom from her. He worked in local foundries to earn the necessary money.

This fugitive slave is being pursued by dogs. Often the animals were specially bred to track and catch runaways.

The Penalties for Aiding Fugitives: The Case of Delia Webster

In 1844, Delia Webster was arrested in Kentucky for aiding fugitives. Born in Vergennes, Vermont, in 1817, Webster had been raised in a family and community with strong antislavery views. She briefly attended Oberlin College in Ohio, where she was further exposed to abolitionist ideas. After teaching school for a short time in Vermont and New York City, she settled in Kentucky to be a teacher. There, she teamed up with Calvin Fairbanks, who had also attended Oberlin College and who since 1837 had regularly transported fugitives across the Ohio River. While attempting to help a fugitive named Lewis Hayden, his wife, Harriet, and their child, they were discovered and arrested. Tried and convicted in Kentucky for aiding escaped slaves, both were sentenced to terms in the Kentucky State Penitentiary (an extremely rare occurrence in southern society for a female offender). On their release, both resumed their illegal activities as Underground Railroad "conductors" and "stationmasters." Webster served two additional jail terms for his activities "aiding and abetting slaves to escape."

The fugitive Hayden family managed to reach Detroit, Michigan, via the Underground Railroad and later moved to Boston. They turned their home in that city into an Underground Railroad station. It is said that they kept two kegs of gunpowder under their front stoop. They greeted bounty hunters at the door with lit candles, saying that they would rather drop the candles and blow up the house than surrender the ex-slaves in their trust. [1]

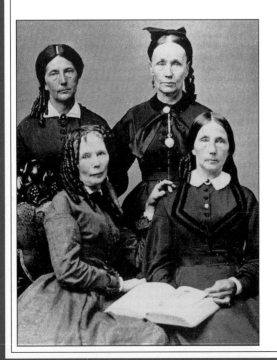

Delia Webster, left foreground, in the only known photograph of her.

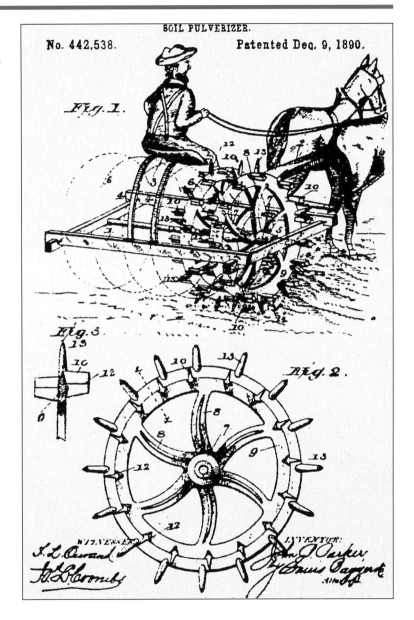

A design for a soil pulverizer, which John Parker, later as a freeman, was able to patent.

At one job, Parker developed a new design for a circular harrow called a clod smasher that could more efficiently loosen the soil in preparation for planting. He made a model of his improved design and proudly showed it to the superintendent of the foundry, who promptly claimed the idea—and the model—as his own. Parker had hoped that profits from

Ozella Williams's Underground Railroad Quilt Code

Using patterns to communicate symbolic meaning was an established tradition in Africa, and it was carried on by slaves in the New World. Blacks used codes to aid escaped slaves by embedding them in quilt patterns. There is even a pattern—the Jacobs' Ladder pattern—that was renamed the Underground Railroad pattern, based on the legend that a quilt in this pattern would be hung outside an Underground Railroad station to signal that it was a safe haven. Legends have long existed about such quilts, but until recently no one had been able to document either them or the codes they conveyed. Then in 1994, quite by chance, a journalist named Jacqueline L. Tobin met a black woman in Charleston, South Carolina. The woman, a quilter named Ozella McDaniel Williams, later shared with Tobin the 150-year-old Underground Railroad quilt code that had been handed down in her family for generations. By following the coded directions, fugitive slaves could make their way safely from South Carolina along the Appalachian mountain range to Cleveland, Ohio, and then on to Canada. Tobin consulted an African-American quilter and quilt historian, Raymond G. Dobard, and together the two embarked on three years of research to document the code handed down in Williams's family. Their research led them to make many connections to African pattern-making and coding. In a book published in 1999 titled *Hidden in Plain View: A Secret Story of Quilts and the Underground Railroad*, Tobin and Dobard revealed the results of their research.

According to Ozella Williams, there were ten quilts used to direct the slaves to take particular actions. Each quilt featured one of the ten patterns. The ten quilts were placed one at a time on a fence, as that was the common way to air them out. Only one quilt would appear at any one time. Each quilt signaled the action that a slave or group of slaves should take at that point on the route.

A log cabin quilt airing in the window of a slave cabin was a secret sign "hidden in plain view."

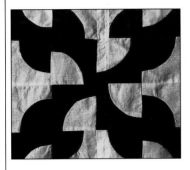

The pattern the drunkard's path told slaves to follow a zigzag path to elude capture.

This is a simplified version of Ozella Williams's quilt code. The words in **boldface** refer to quilter's patterns:

The **monkey wrench** turns the **wagon wheel** toward Canada on a **bear's paw** trail to the **crossroads**.

The monkey wrench pattern was a signal for those slaves who planned to escape to collect the necessary tools they would need for the journey north. The wagon wheel pattern signaled that it was time to pack provisions. The bear's paw pattern told the fugitives to travel through the mountains, which were inhabited by numerous bears, whose well-worn tracks could be followed.

Once they got to the **crossroads** they dug a **log cabin** on the ground.

The crossroads referred to Cleveland, Ohio, the largest city in what was then a free state and a major terminal of the Underground Railroad. "Dug a log cabin in the ground" probably meant drawing a picture in the dirt with a stick. The log cabin may have been a symbol for a safe house or a symbol used to recognize persons with whom it was safe to communicate.

Flying geese stay on the **drunkard's path** and follow the **stars**.

Flying geese referred to the fact that geese fly north in the spring and summer. The drunkard's path quilt pattern was a clear warning to the slaves to follow a zigzag, or staggered, path so as to elude slave catchers. "Drunkards weave back and forth, never moving in a straight line," Ozella Williams explained.[1]

The secret Underground Railroad quilt code revealed by Ozella Williams is the first such code to be documented. There are probably more, and it is hoped that they, too, will be revealed in years to come.

The free states bordering the Ohio River became important iron-processing centers in the nineteenth century. The industrialized North offered great opportunities to talented innovators such as John P. Parker.

his invention would help pay his way out of slavery. He confronted the superintendent and was dismissed from the foundry. Fortunately, a new foundry was opening, and he got work there.

Finally in 1845, after eighteen months of payments, John P. Parker was a freeman. He had learned from talking to people about the North that there were iron foundries in Indiana, and he decided to go there to start his new life. He secured legal documents, called free papers, from the local authorities and sewed them into his clothes. Before he left, he thanked the widow who had made it possible for him to be free and felt some regret at leaving her, since she had treated him well. He also paid a visit to his former owner, the doctor, who advised him not to stop anywhere until he had reached the free states. He later said that "most of my life as a slave was a pleasant one, so far as my bodily wants were concerned. But I hated the injustices and restraints against my own initiative more than it is possible for words to express. To me that was the great curse of slavery." [5]

Running away was often a hard decision. Fugitives left behind family and friends, and there was no guarantee they would make it to freedom.

Four

Harriet Jacobs, Fugitive Slave in the North

WHEN HE WAS STILL A SLAVE, JOHN PARKER HAD DECIDED TO ESCAPE AND had taken off without much preparation. Along the way, at least according to the story he later told, he had asked for help just once. By contrast, a very definite and detailed plan was hatched before Harriet Jacobs emerged from the attic prison she had occupied for seven long years. By following this strategy, she managed to reach Philadelphia, from where the city's vigilant committee assisted her on her journey farther north.

Jacobs's ultimate destination was New York City, where she had friends from Edenton. She would also be close to her daughter, who was then living in the separate city of Brooklyn, across the East River. After about six months with her father in Washington, D.C., Louisa Matilda had been sent to Brooklyn to serve in the household of James Iredell Tredwell, a cousin of her father's. It is possible that the situation of Louisa Matilda serving her own father and half sister had proved uncomfortable for everyone involved.

After staying in Philadelphia a few days, Jacobs and her friend, Hannah Pritchard, boarded a train to New York City. Harriet's grandmother had given her money, so she could afford a first-class ticket. But her Philadelphia friends explained to her that black people were not allowed to ride in the first-class cars. "This was the first chill to my enthusiasm about the Free States," Jacobs later wrote. [1]

There would be more, for white prejudice against blacks was as strong in the free states as it was in the slaveholding areas. According to William Wells Brown, another escaped slave who would write the first novel by an African American, "In the so-called Free States I had been treated as one born to occupy an inferior position; in steamers, compelled to take my fare on the deck; in hotels, to take my meals in the kitchen; in coaches, to ride on the outside; in railways, to ride in the 'Negro car'; and in churches, to sit in the 'Negro pew.'" [2] Jacobs would experience some of the same indignities in the North.

Arriving in New York City, Jacobs was taken aback by the crowd of coachmen competing for customers. Her friends in Philadelphia had given her the name and address of a boardinghouse on Sullivan Street, and she and Hannah took a carriage to it. The New York Anti-Slavery Society had been alerted and provided a home for Hannah, while Harriet contacted friends from Edenton.

Their experience was far different from that of slaves who did not have the same network of friends and connections. For those slaves, New York City was more a stopping-off point than a destination. It had a number of active Underground Railroad stations. In Manhattan, Mother A.M.E. (African Methodist Episcopal) Zion Church, one of the first churches in the city built and led by blacks, doubled as a safe house.

Harriet Jacobs was confronted with a much different world when she arrived in New York City. A view of Broadway in lower Manhattan, 1834.

Another was the home of David Ruggles, leader of the New York Committee of Vigilance and editor of the first black magazine in the United States, *Mirror of Liberty*. In 1838, while living at 36 Lispenard Street, he sheltered Frederick Washington Bailey, who would later take the name Frederick Douglass. The city of Brooklyn and the many towns that made up the county of Queens were much more rural than Manhattan, so traveling in secret was easier. After being in New York a while, Harriet Jacobs probably knew of some of the Underground Railroad stations in those areas.

As soon as she could, Jacobs visited her daughter. To account for all the time that had passed since she had first disappeared nearly seven years

Slave Hunters

Slave hunters ranged far from home to catch fugitives. In one case in 1823, two slave hunters from Kentucky traveled all the way to Lockport, in northern New York State, to find a fugitive. According to a city directory published forty-five years later, the hunters were "dressed in the characteristic leggins of green."

It was in the Fall of 1823, when there were large bodies of Irishmen still engaged excavating rock though the mountain ridge. Darius Comstock, a Quaker, had a large number in his employ on the section he had under contract, and with his brother Joseph, was extensively known as a defender of the fugitive slave from the clutches of the slave-hunter. The two Kentuckians soon pounced on a person by the name of Joseph Pickard, a barber, and arrested him under a warrant issued by Hiram Gardner, then a Justice of the Peace. The arrest was at once noised abroad, and, "Friend Darius," promptly appeared before the Justice with the alleged slave and Kentuckians. A large crowd of the Canal workmen were also on hand, and filled up the street in front of the office of the Justice. The office was in the second story of a wooden building, located near Brown's hat store, and was entered by a flight of stairs on the outside. While the examination was progressing, the prisoner sprang through an open window and landed among the crowd in the street below. The crowd was so great that he could not get away until the Kentuckians rushed down the outside stairs with drawn pistols, and again seized him. The Kentuckians were collared and dared to shoot by G.W. Rogers and others. After a war of words the prisoner, by consent of all parties, went before the Justice again, who, on carefully hearing the case, discharged him for want of proof that he was the property of the persons claiming him. The Kentuckians, from indications by the crowd, concluded it was safest to leave Lockport. Comstock was heard to say that "the prisoner could never be taken away from Lockport by the slave-hunters." [1]

In the South and the North, in slavery and in freedom, the care of white children was a common role for countless black women.

earlier, she told the Tredwells that she had been in Canada. She was surprised and troubled to learn that her daughter had not been sent to school after all, even though there was an African Free School on Nassau Street not far away. And she was shocked when the woman of the house told her that Louisa Matilda's father had "given" the child to her oldest daughter to be her waiting maid when she grew up.

In spite of not having references from any previous employers, Jacobs managed to get a job caring for the infant of Nathaniel Parker Willis and his English-born wife, Mary. She moved into the Astor House, where the family resided. The five-story hotel on the west side of Broadway between Barclay and Vesey Streets had been erected between 1834 and 1836, the first luxury hotel in the city. It boasted more than three hundred guest rooms and was one of the most opulent hotels in the city. The years of living in a cramped space had caused Jacobs's legs to swell, and it was painful for her to go up and down stairs. Her employer sympathized and summoned a doctor to care for her. Jacobs saw her daughter as often as she could and looked forward to the time when they could live together.

One morning as she was looking out the window, Jacobs recognized her brother, John. He was living in Boston, Massachusetts, and working as a sailor but was in New York on a visit. They had a joyous, tearful reunion.

Jacobs saved her earnings and hoped to purchase her freedom. But when she wrote to her young mistress back in Edenton, her request was denied. Not long afterward, she received a letter from a friend in Edenton advising her that Dr. Norcom was about to travel to New York. Fearing that he meant to recapture her, Jacobs arranged to visit her brother in Boston.

While she was in Boston, her son Joseph was sent to her. (Joseph had been left in the care of her grandmother, who apparently believed that his father, Samuel Tredwell Sawyer, planned to free him and would not object to his going north.) It was agreed that Joseph would live in

A runaway slave is treed by a group of men on horseback and their dogs.

Boston with his uncle John, since Harriet had no home of her own. Meanwhile, in New York City, Dr. Norcom tried and failed to find Jacobs. As soon as she heard that he had gone back to Edenton, Jacobs returned to the city and her job in the Willis household.

But Jacobs was in danger from people other than Dr. Norcom. New York City was crawling with slave hunters. By the middle 1840s, as the abolitionist movement grew in strength and more and more slaves ran away, southern slave owners took harsher steps to stop the rising number of fugitives. In addition to offering rewards and advertising for the return of fugitives on posters and in newspapers, many hired slave hunters, also called slave catchers, blackbirders, and bounty hunters. These men made their living by hunting down fugitive slaves and collecting the rewards offered by slaveholders for the return of their human property. Advertisements offering rewards for the capture of runaway slaves abounded in both southern and northern newspapers and were posted around the docks of port cities and train stations and post offices.

In 1844, Jacobs had another scare. She learned that a relative of the Tredwells, who were keeping Louisa Matilda, had written to Dr. Norcom, giving him Jacobs's address and offering to help in her recapture. She felt she had no choice but to tell her employer that she was a fugitive slave and to ask for help. Mrs. Willis understood her plight and drove her in her carriage to the home of one of her friends, where she could stay temporarily.

Harriet contacted members of the New York Vigilance Committee, who advised her to go to Boston to stay with her brother. They sent word to John Jacobs, who arranged to go to New York to get his sister in a few days. Harriet decided to take Louisa Matilda to Boston with her, securing the Tredwells' permission to take her to Boston for a brief visit.

Harriet, John, and Louisa Matilda Jacobs traveled to Boston by passenger steamer. Harriet purchased the tickets. Although as a rule, black passengers were not allowed to sleep in the cabin, the captain made an exception for Harriet and her daughter. They arrived in Boston without incident. Harriet and Louisa Matilda found lodging with a friend, and Harriet supported herself and her daughter as a dressmaker.

Jacobs's son, Joseph, now lived in Boston with John Jacobs, so for the first time in nearly nine years Harriet had both her children with her. She later wrote, "I watched them with a swelling heart. Their every motion delighted me."[3] She was pleased with Joseph's progress in school, but concerned that Louisa Matilda had not been taught to read and write. Rather than send her daughter to school with Joseph, she taught Louisa Matilda at home until she was ready to enter an intermediate school.

In the North, blacks were segregated on most modes of transportation, assigned to the decks of steamships and to separate railway cars.

In the spring of 1845, Jacobs received word that her kind employer, Mrs. Willis, had died. Mr. Willis wanted to take their little daughter, Imogen, to England to visit his late wife's family, and he asked Jacobs to accompany them. She spent ten months in England with the Willis family, which was longer than she had planned.

On her return to Boston, Jacobs learned that her son had gone to sea. Apprenticed to a printer, seventeen-year-old Joseph had gotten along fine with his fellow apprentices until, as Jacobs later recalled, "one day they accidentally discovered a fact they had never before suspected—that he was colored! This at once transformed him into a different being. Some of the apprentices were Americans, others American-born Irish; and it was offensive to their dignity to have a 'nigger' among them, after they had been told that he *was* a 'nigger.'"[4] Offended by this ill treatment merely because of his race, Joseph had shipped out on a whaling voyage.

In 1848, Harriet's brother, John, decided to move to Rochester, New York, where there was a strong antislavery movement. He offered to pay Louisa Matilda's tuition at a nearby boarding school. Although Harriet hated to part with her daughter so soon after her return from England, she wanted her child to continue her education. Louisa Matilda was enrolled at the Young Ladies Domestic Seminary in Clinton, New York. It was a racially integrated school, founded by the abolitionist Hiram H. Kellogg. Kellogg offered black students reduced rates under an arrangement whereby he paid half their expenses and another abolitionist, the wealthy Gerrit Smith, paid the rest.

Not long afterward, Jacobs received a letter from her young mistress. Mary Matilda Norcom had married a man named Daniel Messmore, and she wanted Harriet to come back to Virginia to live with them. In the letter, Mary Matilda stated that she knew Harriet had been abroad and was now back in New York. Harriet again began to worry about her own safety. Her brother, John, asked her to join him in Rochester and help him operate an antislavery reading room. She was grateful for the opportunity. She moved to Rochester in the spring of 1849. Although the reading room was not a success, she stayed on to be close to her daughter and once again found work as a dressmaker.

In Rochester, Jacobs found herself in a major center of abolitionism, as well as the last major stop on the Underground Railroad in northwestern New York. Situated on Lake Ontario, the city was an ideal point from which to sail across the lake to Canada and freedom. There was an active branch of the Female Anti-Slavery Society in Rochester. Its members included Susan B. Anthony and Amy Post, both outspoken activists for women's rights as well as for the rights of slaves to be treated as

An 1845 antislavery meeting in Cazenovia, New York, was attended by Frederick Douglass, right, and Gerrit Smith, standing behind Douglass.

human beings. Frederick Douglass, whose *Narrative of the Life of Frederick Douglass, an American Slave, Written by Himself* had been published in 1845, was living in Rochester. In 1847, he had begun publication of an antislavery newspaper, *The North Star*, in the city. In the first issue, Douglass asserted that he was involved in the operation of the Underground Railroad.

Harriet Jacobs did not remain in Rochester long. Her brother, having failed to make a success of the antislavery reading room, returned to New York City. She would soon follow, arriving in the city in the same month Congress passed a new fugitive slave law that called for harsher penalties for runaway slaves and the people who aided them. Her freedom was again at risk.

Her brother was not in danger. He had not run from a slave state, but had been brought to a free state by his master. John Jacobs decided to go to the newly admitted free state of California. The discovery of gold in California in 1848 had excited the imagination of thousands, leading to the gold rush of 1849. John wanted to pan for gold in the hope of getting rich. Harriet's son, Joseph, wanted to go to California with his uncle, and she agreed to let him go. Louisa Matilda was still attending school in Clinton, where she was busy and popular and not much company for her mother. Preferring to be with people who knew her, Harriet accepted the invitation of her former employer to rejoin his household. Nathaniel Parker Willis had remarried, and there was a new baby for Harriet to tend, as well as the older girl, Imogen, whom she had cared for from infancy.

Dr. James Norcom died in Edenton in November 1850. Communications were much slower in that era, and Jacobs did not learn of his death until the following spring. In the meantime, aware that he had made new plans for her recapture, she fled to Massachusetts, where she hid for a month. Even after she learned of Norcom's death, she knew she was not safe. Her actual owner, Mary Matilda Messmore, had inherited her

This cartoon, entitled "Effects of the Fugitive-Slave-Law" criticized the 1850 act.

father's stubbornness about taking back what was rightfully hers. In 1852, Mary Messmore traveled to New York to catch Jacobs, who had to go into hiding in Massachusetts once again. Her ordeal finally ended when her employer arranged to purchase her. Through an agent, the second Mrs. Willis offered $300 to Mary Matilda's husband, Daniel Messmore. When Messmore said that amount was too small, the agent reminded him that it was better than nothing, for Jacobs had friends who would spirit her out of the country, if necessary. Messmore accepted the offer. These negotiations took place without Jacobs's knowledge, for Jacobs was against the notion of buying and selling human beings. "A human being *sold* in the free city of New York!" she later wrote. "I had objected to having my freedom bought, yet I must confess that when it was done I felt as if a heavy load had been lifted from my weary shoulders. When I rode home in the cars I was no longer afraid to unveil my face and look at people as they passed." [5]

The Fugitive Slave Act of 1850

Passed after aggressive lobbying by southern Congressmen, the new fugitive slave law was one of a series of bills that made up the so-called Compromise of 1850, adopted on September 9 of that year. The law was a response to years of efforts by many northerners to aid fugitive slaves.

Back in 1826, the Quaker stronghold of Pennsylvania had passed an anti-kidnapping law. Under that law, in 1837, a slave hunter named Edward Prigg was convicted of kidnapping an escaped slave named Mary Morgan and her two children and returning them to their owner in Maryland. Prigg had not bothered to get a warrant for Morgan's arrest, and therefore he was guilty of kidnapping. Prigg's attorneys appealed his conviction to the U.S. Supreme Court. They argued that Prigg's actions were justified under the provisions of the Fugitive Slave Act of 1793. The Supreme Court handed down its decision in the case of *Prigg v. Pennsylvania* in 1842. The decision sent mixed signals: On the one hand, it upheld the law of 1793 and ruled that a slaveholder's right to his property overrode any state legislation to the contrary. However, the court also held that it was the federal government's responsibility to enforce the fugitive slave clause of the Constitution and that states need not cooperate in any way.

Many northern states viewed that second part of the court's ruling as a signal to pass new personal liberty laws that barred the use of state authorities or property in the recapture of fugitives. Nine states passed such laws between 1842 and 1850. Southern slave owners were furious over this turn of events, and they pressed their legislators to do something. Congress was then trying to decide whether to admit new states to the Union as slave or free states. Within the Compromise of 1850, California, Utah, and New Mexico were admitted to the Union, California as a free state and the other two as free or slave depending on the constitutions they wrote. To appease pro-slavery members of Congress, the bill also included the Fugitive Slave Act of 1850. It strengthened the provisions of the Fugitive Slave Act of 1793 by requiring citizens to assist in the recovery of fugitive slaves. It denied a fugitive's right to a jury trial. (Cases would instead be handled by special commissioners who would be paid $5 if an alleged fugitive were released and $10 if he or she were returned to the person claiming ownership.) It also called for more federal officials to enforce the law.

Southern slave owners and slave catchers were quick to take advantage of the new federal support they received. In New York City, a black man named James Hamlet became the first victim. Harriet Jacobs wrote that he was "given up by the bloodhounds of the north to the bloodhounds of the south." She continued, "It was the beginning of a reign of terror to the colored population. The great city rushed on in its whirl of excitement. . . . But while fashionables were listening to the thrilling voice of Jenny Lind in Metropolitan Hall, the thrilling voices of poor hunted colored people went up, in an agony of supplication, to the Lord, from Zion's church." [1] She was referring to a protest meeting at Zion Chapel Street Church on October 1, 1850, attended by more than 1,500 people, most of them black. Harriet's brother, John, spoke to the crowd and proposed that they begin a registry of slave catchers, so they could quickly identify them and track their activities. He also urged armed defiance of the law. The assembled group raised $800 to buy Hamlet's freedom. Four days later, on October 5, many of those same people participated in a huge victory celebration welcoming him back to the city.

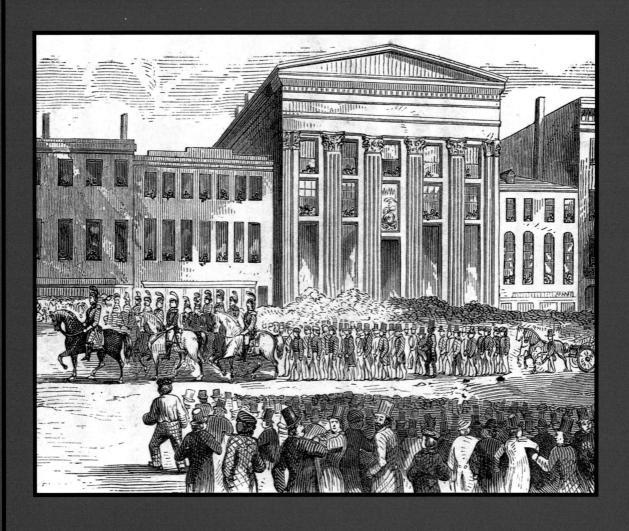

This engraving depicts a federal marshal on horseback leading a posse down State Street in Boston after the capture of fugitive slave Anthony Burns.

Five

John P. Parker, Underground Railroad Conductor

BY THE TIME THE 1850 FUGITIVE SLAVE ACT WAS PASSED, JOHN P. PARKER had become a conductor on the Underground Railroad. He had first helped runaways in 1845, not long after he had purchased his freedom and gone north to Cincinnati, Ohio. He was working as an iron molder and staying in a boardinghouse. One of his fellow boarders was a barber who was a freeman. He had lived in Maysville, Kentucky, but had left after being accused of helping runaways. Just before his departure, he had been asked by two young slave girls to help them escape. He had refused. Safe in Cincinnati, he regretted not having helped the girls and asked Parker to go to Kentucky with him to rescue them. Parker was happy and content in his new life and had no interest in risking his own safety for someone

An illustration of Maysville, Kentucky, as it looked in the mid-1840s.

else. But the barber persisted, and eventually Parker agreed to help.

The two traveled to Ripley, Ohio, just over the Kentucky border. They tried to find a boat to steal and row across the Ohio River. After three nights of looking for a boat without success, the barber gave up. Parker, however, did not. He recalled years later, "Having set my face towards a goal, I was determined to make another try at it, even if I had to go alone."[1] Unlike the barber, Parker was not known in Maysville, so he traveled there and located a friend of the barber's who lived in a settlement of freemen. The barber's friend told him where to find a boat and agreed to bring the two girls to meet him.

Long before daybreak, the girls were brought to Parker. He was astonished to see that they wore layers and layers of dresses and hoop skirts and were carrying what appeared to be all their earthly belongings. He refused to carry so much baggage, fearing that the boat would sink. He then rowed the ten miles to the Ohio side of the river. As he approached the Ohio shore, he heard the sounds of oars behind him and realized that someone had seen the bundles left back on the other shore and taken off after him in another boat. He got as near the shore as he could, where one of the girls leaped out of the boat, upsetting it and dumping Parker into the water. He clambered ashore and helped the second girl to land. The three scrambled through a cornfield, then hid in the woods as daylight broke. They spent the day in hiding, and shortly after dark made their way to the black settlement just outside Ripley. There he learned that the whole town had heard of the escape and that officers had searched for the fugitives and were still on the watch. At the suggestion of one of the settlement's residents, Parker took the girls to hide under a bridge. At midnight, they were escorted to the home of a local abolitionist and stationmaster on the Underground Railroad. That man, Eli Collins, agreed to shelter the girls. "That," recalled John Parker years later, "was my forcible introduction to Ripley and the Underground Railroad."[2]

Seeing the girls to freedom altogether changed Parker's outlook. He felt it was his mission to help fugitive slaves. He began to lead a double life, going about his usual business by day and risking his own safety to aid escaped slaves at night. In 1848, he met and married Miranda Boulden, and the two started a family. He continued to work in the iron trades and also opened a small general store in the nearby black town of Beechwood Factory, Ohio. In 1849, he moved his family to Ripley, Ohio, which was a center for flatboat building and a hub of the Underground Railroad activity.

Parker became a conductor on the Underground Railroad. He later asserted that by the time the Fugitive Slave Act of 1850 was passed, he had assisted 315 runaways. He had kept a diary of his adventures, includ-

A slave family gathers in front of their cabin in rural Kentucky. Freedom lay just across the Ohio River.

ing the names, dates, and circumstances of each incident. But the new law was stringent in punishing those who helped fugitives. Parker had acquired property. He had opened his own iron foundry on the bank of the river and had bought a house next door. He did not want it confiscated. There were many people in Ripley who were against the Underground Railroad activity in their town, and Parker was afraid of being reported. He did not wish to be found with evidence of his secret nighttime adventures. So, he threw the diary into the iron furnace at his foundry. But he did not halt his Underground Railroad activity.

In his autobiography, Parker detailed many adventures. Although most of his work involved shuttling fugitives out of Ripley and on to the next stop on the Underground Railroad, there were occasions when he left Ripley. He once undertook the daring rescue of a party of ten fugitives who were hiding deep in the Kentucky woods and afraid to continue after their leader had been captured. Finding the group, Parker endeavored to lead them safely out of the woods to the river. He lost one man who wandered off in search of water and was captured by slave catchers. But he reached the river with the other nine. As the baying of hounds grew closer by the second, he piled the group into his boat, only to find that it would not hold everyone. He ordered two men to remain behind. But a woman began to wail that one of them was her husband. Parker recalled, "Then I witnessed an example of heroism and self-sacrifice that made me proud of my race. For one of the single men safely in the boat, hearing the cry of the woman for her husband, arose without a word [and] walked quietly to the bank. The husband sprang into the boat as I pushed off." [3] As Parker rowed away in the darkness, he saw lights and heard shouts back on shore and knew that the men had been captured.

One of Parker's most exciting and dangerous adventures was rescuing a Kentucky slave couple and their infant child. Parker was the one who initiated this particular escape. On a dare, he traveled across the river to Kentucky, secretly made contact with the couple, and arranged to

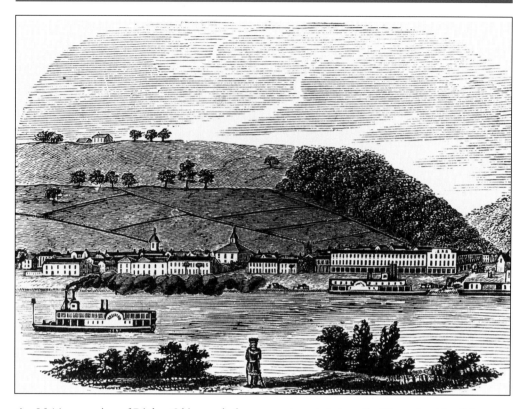

An 1846 engraving of Ripley, Ohio, made from a vantage point on the Kentucky side of the Ohio River.

return a few days later to rescue them. When he did so, the couple refused to go. They had been under suspicion since his last visit, and in an effort to prevent any attempted escape, their owner had demanded the couple bring their infant to his house each night. The baby was placed at the foot of the bed. A lighted candle and two pistols were laid out on a chair beside the sleeping owner. Naturally, the couple would not leave without their baby.

Parker tried to talk the parents into rescuing the baby themselves, but they were too frightened of the master and his guns. Rather than return to Ripley empty-handed, Parker decided to get the baby himself. He questioned the woman, who worked as a house servant, about the interior of the house and the bedroom. He then told the couple to pack up their belongings and leave, arranging to meet them at a spot some distance away from the farm. He took off his shoes and handed them to the man, telling him to destroy the shoes if anything happened to him.

Parker quietly stole into the house and made his way to the bedroom, leaving doors open as he went along so he could make a quick escape. He was in the bedroom, dragging the sleeping bundle that was the baby toward him, when the bedroom door swung shut, creating a draft that blew out the candle flame. According to Parker, "There was no cause for secrecy now, so I jumped to my feet and rushed to the door. I heard the stool upset and the pistols fall. I heard the quick breathing of the man as he sprung out of bed and began feeling around on the floor in the dark for his weapons. Opening the door with a jerk, I ran across the kitchen out into the yard, with the bundle still in my arms. From their position in the room the man and woman saw me hurry out of the house, toward the road." [4]

Parker met up with the baby's parents, led them to the boat he had used to cross the river to Kentucky, and rowed them over to Ripley. He was dismayed to learn that in the excitement of the getaway the man had dropped his shoes. If found, they would prove he had been involved in the incident. He left the slave family with an attorney friend, who would hide them and get them to their next stop on the Underground Railroad. Then he went home.

Soon, men arrived to search his house. They were disappointed to find no evidence that he had harbored the fugitives there. The next day a man entered his foundry dangling Parker's lost shoes over his arm. After Parker denied that the shoes were his, the man went from store to store in town, trying to find out who had sold the shoes. Fortunately for Parker, the merchant who had done so did not inform on him.

In his autobiography, Parker reported that authorities in Mason County, Kentucky, offered a $1,000 reward for him, dead or alive, and

A standoff between fugitive slave Margaret Garner and the four men who pursued her. Two of her four children lie dead on the floor, killed by their own mother so they would not have to return to the yoke of slavery.

that he did not believe it until he saw a notice nailed to a tree and read it with his own eyes. Soon, he realized he was being watched. He and his fellow conductors and stationmasters on the Underground Railroad met and decided that for the time being he should cease his activities. Eventually, however, he grew tired of constantly being watched. One night he waited in ambush for the man assigned to watch him and threatened him with a knife, frightening the man away for good.

Still the harassment did not stop. Once while traveling down the river from a town north of Ripley, a group of men from Maysville, Kentucky, tried to keep Parker from going ashore at Ripley. The next stop was Maysville, and they intended to capture and imprison him there. Parker barely escaped by stealing one of the ship's small boats.

Parker's life as a conductor became a series of close calls. Slave owners and slave catchers were not his only concern. He also had to be wary of paid informants, whom he referred to as spies. In one case, he was almost caught hiding two slaves in his house. The two were from southern Kentucky and had managed to reach Ripley before they were captured. Their captor, a Ripley man and a paid informant, had been on the way to the town marshall's office with them when a group of black freemen overpowered him and forcibly rescued the fugitives. They took the two escaped slaves to Parker's house. Meanwhile, the Ripley spy had met up with an armed crowd from across the river who were in pursuit of a different group of runaways. He persuaded them to accompany him to Parker's house. They knew he was not harboring the slaves they sought, but they also knew he had helped other slaves in the past. This was an opportunity to get even with him. The armed group forced their way into his house and began to search it. As loudly as he could, Parker told the slave catchers that they were free to search every nook and cranny, even the roof. He hoped the two runaways, who were hiding in the attic, would hear him and make their way to the roof. They did so. The catchers failed to include the roof in their search, so Parker and his two charges were safe for the time being. Eventually, Parker got the two fugitives out of Ripley by way of a friend's carpentry shop. The friend, Tom Collins, was also a worker on the Underground Railroad. He built coffins and often hid fugitives in the unfinished coffins in his shop. That time, both Parker and the fugitives hid in Collins's coffins until the slave catchers had searched the rest of the premises and departed. According to Parker, "Though they examined the shop, and cupboard particularly, they did not in that gloom care to touch the row of coffins, feeling assured that no colored man would ever consign his living body to such a place of concealment." [5]

Another time, Parker was roused about midnight by a black man who said he was a slave from Kentucky. He asked for help rescuing his wife, who was to be sold the next day. Parker's wife was suspicious and insisted on calling in a white neighbor who sometimes engaged in Underground Railroad activity. Parker and his neighbor threatened the slave and eventually forced him to admit that he had been sent as a decoy by his owner. His owner and three other men were lying in wait down-river, determined to capture Parker and collect the $1,000 reward.

Parker decided to teach the slave owner and his friends a lesson. Although the slave pleaded to return to his owner, Parker instructed his neighbor to take him to the local black settlement of Red Oak. Then Parker armed himself with two pistols and a knife, and with his large dog set off along the shore. When he found the four men's hiding place, he called to them that he knew where they were. They emerged and demanded to know where their man was. "What man?" asked Parker innocently. Eventually, they confessed that they had sent a slave as a decoy. Parker replied that he had seen a runaway at his house and as far as he knew the fugitive was on his way to Canada. Upon his return, Parker discovered that the reluctant runaway had indeed decided to escape and agreed to go on from Red Oak via the Underground Railroad to Canada.

For those who had lived their lives enslaved, freedom was a powerful lure. For John Parker, former slave and courageous adventurer, the urge to help fugitives was strong as well. There is no telling how long he would have continued as an Underground Railroad conductor if the Civil War had not intervened to bring the railroad's business to an end.

The John P. Parker House in a photograph from 1910. The home fronted the Ohio River.

The home of Thomas Collins, cabinet and coffin maker, as shown in this 1910 photograph.

135,000 SETS, 270,000 VOLUMES SOLD.

UNCLE TOM'S CABIN

FOR SALE HERE.

AN EDITION FOR THE MILLION, COMPLETE IN 1 Vol., PRICE 37 1-2 CENTS.
"   "   IN GERMAN, IN 1 Vol., PRICE 50 CENTS.
"   "   IN 2 Vols,. CLOTH, 6 PLATES, PRICE $1.50.
SUPERB ILLUSTRATED EDITION, IN 1 Vol., WITH 153 ENGRAVINGS,
PRICES FROM $2.50 TO $5.00.

The Greatest Book of the Age.

Harriet Beecher Stowe's Uncle Tom's Cabin *became a sensation, and sales of the novel were brisk.*

Six

The Gathering Clouds of War

WHILE JOHN PARKER WAS AIDING FUGITIVE SLAVES, EVENTS IN THE 1850s slowly advanced the nation toward civil war. It was a decade of unrest and growing animosity on both sides of the slavery question. No one had been happy with the Fugitive Slave Law that had been part of the Compromise of 1850. Slaveholders tried to have the law strictly enforced, and abolitionists were just as determined to ignore its provisions.

The publication of an antislavery novel, *Uncle Tom's Cabin*, in 1852 hastened the conflict. Its author, Harriet Beecher Stowe, was moved to write about slavery and the Underground Railroad after the Fugitive Slave Act was passed. Stowe based her story on real people and events. The Uncle Tom in her story was Josiah Henson, who escaped with his family from Kentucky, crossed the Ohio River into Indiana, and traveled from there to Cincinnati. He was helped by a tribe of Indians to reach Sandusky, Ohio, boarded a Scottish steamer to Buffalo, New York, and

This lithograph entitled The Flight of Eliza *captures a pivotal scene in Stowe's* Uncle Tom's Cabin.

from there traveled to Canada. The Eliza in Stowe's story was a young Kentucky slave woman who had fled with her baby in the dead of winter. Pursued by slave catchers, she had crossed the treacherous Ohio River by hopping from one ice floe to another. Reaching the other side, she had been helped to the home of the Reverend John Rankin, with whom John P. Parker often worked. From there, she traveled via the Underground Railroad to Sandusky, then crossed Lake Erie into Canada.

Uncle Tom's Cabin was an instant best-seller in the United States and was eventually translated into twenty-three languages. Hailed by abolitionists as proof of the evils of slavery, it was regarded as poison by pro-slavery forces. Even possessing a copy of the book was a crime in the slave states. Frederick Douglass had his own criticisms of the book. He charged that

Stowe and others who wrote about the brave men and women who worked on or traveled on the Underground Railroad were revealing too many secrets. They had made it "The *Upper*-ground Railroad." Douglass claimed, "In publishing such accounts, the anti-slavery man addresses the slaveholder, *not the slave*; he stimulates the former to greater watchfulness, and adds to his facilities for capturing his slave."[1]

In 1854, two years after the publication of *Uncle Tom's Cabin*, the Kansas–Nebraska Act was passed. This legislation provided that the residents of the two territories—they were not yet states—could make their own decisions on the question of slavery. Especially in Kansas, pro- and antislavery forces struggled for control of the territorial government, with the antislavery side eventually winning. Opponents of the Kansas–Nebraska Act formed the new Republican Party, and by 1865 it was well launched in the North.

Three years after the Kansas–Nebraska Act, the U.S. Supreme Court handed down a controversial and seemingly proslavery decision in *Scott v. Sandford*. The case concerned Dred Scott, a Missouri slave who claimed that he was free because his master had taken him to a free state. The Court ruled that Scott was not a citizen and thus had no right to bring suit in the courts. Abolitionists were shocked and dismayed by the decision. But Frederick Douglass predicted that some good would come of it. He wrote, "This very attempt to blot out forever the hopes of an enslaved people may be one necessary link in the chain of events preparatory to the complete overthrow of the whole slave system."[2]

At the time he wrote those words, Douglass knew of at least one plot to overthrow the system. John Brown, born in Connecticut and raised in Ohio, was an ardent abolitionist. He later moved to Richmond, Pennsylvania, where he established an Underground Railroad station. In the late 1840s, he moved to New York State, purchasing 244 acres adjacent to a settlement called Timbucto, a remarkable experiment in black land ownership in the North.

The abolitionist John Brown. He justified his acts of violence by saying that he was an instrument in the hand of God.

Timbucto had been established on property purchased by a wealthy white abolitionist named Gerrit Smith in 1846. Smith, who was a supporter of the school in Clinton, New York, that Louisa Matilda Jacobs attended, had made the purchase to enable black men to vote. Back in 1821, a law had been passed in New York State that denied black men the right to vote unless they owned $250 worth of land. Only black men had to meet this qualification. White men could vote if they owned property valued at a mere $100. This law effectively eliminated the vote for black men even after slavery ended in New York in 1827.

Smith owned 750,000 acres in New York. He decided to give some of his land to worthy African Americans, and with the help of the Reverend Henry Highland Garnet, a black New York abolitionist, he distributed parcels of land worth $250. The new landowners were thus qualified to vote. Soon many black families were headed north to claim their land. Around North Elba, New York, they established Timbucto.

John Brown moved his family to the area, determined to help the black settlers. Although Brown himself was soon spending most of his time traveling in connection with his wool production business, his family of ten stayed on the land and built their farmhouse with the assistance of one of the black residents of Timbucto. Three of Brown's daughters married fugitive slaves from Maryland, who had settled in the area because they felt safe there.

After the passage of the Kansas–Nebraska Act in 1854, Brown set out from North Elba with his sons to prevent the territory of Kansas from becoming a slave state. Although his son Frederick was killed in the struggle, antislavery forces won out, and Kansas was admitted to the Union as a free state. Returning to New York, Brown began to meet with important abolitionists to discuss a daring plan to free a large number of slaves. He would establish a stronghold in the mountains of Virginia and send out a call to nearby slaves to join him. He would then assist them in escaping north to Canada. By April 1858, he had contacted Harriet Tubman, the most famous conductor on the Underground Railroad. She had bought a house for her parents, whom she had rescued from slavery, in Auburn, New York, and visited them from time to time. She herself divided her time between the town of Saint Catharines in Ontario, Canada, and Cape May, New Jersey, and made two trips a year back to Maryland to lead slaves north to freedom. Brown wanted Tubman's assistance in helping him get the slaves he would gather in Virginia to Canada. She agreed to help him and met with him several times to advise him of the routes she knew and the hiding places along the way, even

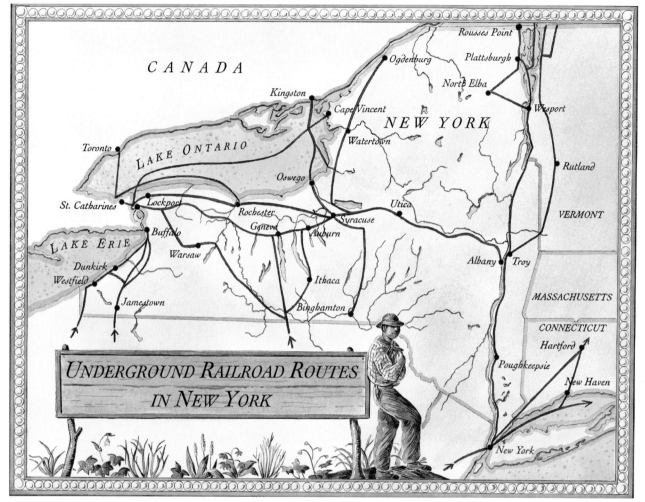

New York State was crisscrossed with an extensive network of Underground Railroad routes. By land or by water, thousands of fugitive slaves were shuttled out of harm's way.

drawing rough maps for him. By contrast, Frederick Douglass and some other New York abolitionists considered Brown's plan too dangerous and would have nothing to do with it.

Brown enlisted twenty-two men, of whom seventeen were whites, including his own sons. They made their way to Virginia and scouted out a suitable mountain stronghold. Deciding that his band would need more

Harriet Tubman was known as the "Moses of Her People." Having escaped herself, she knew firsthand the horrors of slavery.

A large crowd witnessed the execution of two men who had participated in the raid on Harpers Ferry led by John Brown.

arms and ammunition to carry out the plan, on October 16 and 18, 1859, Brown led an attack on the United States arsenal at Harpers Ferry, Virginia. Federal troops commanded by Colonel Robert E. Lee put down the assault, killing ten men in the process, two of whom were Brown's sons. Brown himself was captured. In early December, he was hanged. His body was taken back to North Elba, New York, for burial. The place became a shrine for those who opposed slavery.

Considered a martyr by antislavery forces, and a madman by proslavery people, Brown's action and his resulting execution prompted many people who had not yet taken sides on the slavery question to do so. By the time of the 1860 presidential election, no more compromises were possible. Antislavery factions voted for the Republican candidate, Abraham Lincoln, who was elected the sixteenth president of the United States.

Lincoln was not an abolitionist. In fact, he had mixed feelings about slavery. But the South viewed his election as the final insult. Within a month, South Carolina seceded from the Union, soon followed by Alabama, Florida, Georgia, Louisiana, Mississippi, and Texas. Lincoln was sworn in as president of a nation that now consisted of seven fewer states than when he had been elected. Those seven states formed a new union called the Confederate States of America. On April 12, 1861, Confederate forces fired on federal Fort Sumter in Charleston, South Carolina, and the Civil War began.

Underground Railroad operations slowed after the war broke out. It was not safe for conductors such as Harriet Tubman to venture into slave country to rescue bondmen and -women. The Underground Railroad continued to operate in the North as best it could, for fugitives still managed to get out of the South and still needed help in reaching Canada. As long as slavery continued to exist, there was a role for the Underground Railroad to play, and slavery did not end until the Confederacy was vanquished.

Lydia Maria Child, a New York abolitionist and feminist, encouraged Harriet Jacobs to record her life story.

Seven

Rediscovering the Underground Railroad

As civil war loomed, Harriet Jacobs began to write her life story. She was urged to do so by Amy Post, a prominent New York abolitionist and women's rights advocate. Post introduced Jacobs to Lydia Maria Child, another New York abolitionist and feminist. Child offered to edit the manuscript and to help get it published. Jacobs remained in the employ of the Willis family and in 1853 moved with them to Cornwall, New York. She hoped someday to have her own home and her children with her. She also hoped to see her grandmother again. This was not to happen. In the same year she started writing her autobiography, her grandmother died in Edenton. Jacobs also received word that her son and his uncle had gone to Australia to look for gold. In 1863, she responded to an appeal from her son, who had fallen ill there, but she never heard from him again. Her brother eventually returned to the United States.

Jacobs completed her manuscript at the beginning of 1858. She titled it *Incidents in the Life of a Slave Girl, Written By Herself.* She used the pseudonym, or pen name, Linda Brent and changed the names of everyone mentioned. She did so both to protect the people who were close to her and to avoid lawsuits by those who had mistreated her and might claim otherwise. Not long after she finished the manuscript, prominent abolitionists helped finance her trip to England in the hope of finding a publisher for her book. She was unsuccessful and returned to the United States in the fall of 1858. In 1861, at just about the same time as Confederate troops fired on Fort Sumter, Jacobs paid a Boston publisher to print her book.

After the Civil War ended with the surrender of the Confederate forces in April 1865, Jacobs traveled to her hometown of Edenton, North Carolina, to bring relief supplies to the former slaves in the town. She and her daughter, Louisa Matilda, also did relief work in Alexandria, Virginia, and Savannah, Georgia. In 1868, they sailed to London to raise money for a black orphanage and home for the aged in Savannah. By 1870, she had relocated to Cambridge, Massachusetts, to be near her brother, John. She ran a boardinghouse there. John S. Jacobs died in 1875. Ten years later, Harriet and her daughter were living in Washington, D.C. Louisa Matilda Jacobs helped organize the National Association of Colored Women in the district. Harriet Jacobs died there in 1897 and was buried in Mount Auburn Cemetery in Cambridge, Massachusetts.

Over the years, Harriet Jacobs's autobiography, *Incidents in the Life of a Slave Girl*, fell into obscurity. Anyone who read it dismissed it as a false slave narrative that had actually been written by Lydia Maria Child. Jean Fagin Yellin, a professor of English interested in women's studies, thought so, too, when she first read the book in the mid-1970s. Later, as

The title page of the first edition of Incidents in the Life of a Slave Girl, *published in 1861.*

INCIDENTS

IN THE

LIFE OF A SLAVE GIRL.

WRITTEN BY HERSELF.

"Northerners know nothing at all about Slavery. They think it is perpetual bondage only. They have no conception of the depth of *degradation* involved in that word, SLAVERY; if they had, they would never cease their efforts until so horrible a system was overthrown."   A WOMAN OF NORTH CAROLINA.

"Rise up, ye women that are at ease! Hear my voice, ye careless daughters! Give ear unto my speech."
                                                             ISAIAH xxxii. 9.

EDITED BY L. MARIA CHILD.

BOSTON:
PUBLISHED FOR THE AUTHOR.
1861.

she was doing research on black and white antislavery feminists, she came across the book again. This time she reconsidered her initial assessment. Her study of Lydia Maria Child's papers led her to suspect that Linda

Brent had been a real person. Yellin spent years documenting the people and incidents in the book. In 1987, Harvard University Press, located not far from Jacobs's grave in Cambridge, Massachusetts, brought out a new edition of *Incidents*, edited by Yellin and complete with all the evidence Yellin had unearthed proving the existence of Harriet Jacobs. Ninety years after her death, Harriet Jacobs's story was told again, this time to a generation far removed from the realities of slavery. A new paperback edition, published in 2000, includes John Jacobs's memoir.

John P. Parker's work on the Underground Railroad came to an end with the outbreak of the Civil War, but his activism continued for a time. He helped to raise a regiment of escaped slaves to assist the Union forces. In December 1865, eight months after the war ended, he and a partner bought a foundry and blacksmith's shop. He later added on a coal yard and took a partnership in a mill. But the milling business almost bankrupted him. On May 1, 1886, a fire destroyed the mill. Parker rebuilt and named the new foundry and woodworking shop that he opened in 1890 the Phoenix Foundry, after the mythical bird that rises from the ashes. In December of that year, he secured a patent for a new soil pulverizer. He later patented a tobacco press. He was one of only fifty-five black Americans to receive government patents before 1901. When he died in 1900, his will stipulated that none of his six children carry on the family business. He wanted them to get college educations and enter professions, which they did.

In the 1880s, a reporter for the *Chattanooga* (Tennessee) *News* named Frank M. Gregg interviewed Parker as part of his research into Underground Railroad activity in Ripley, Ohio. He took down Parker's recollections and produced a handwritten manuscript that he titled "The Autobiography of John P. Parker." The manuscript was never published and eventually landed in the archives of Duke University in Durham, North Carolina, along with other papers related to the Reverend John Rankin, the more famous Ripley abolitionist.

John P. Parker's house (right) and his Phoenix Foundry (left) in a photograph taken some time in the second half of the nineteenth century.

In the parts of Ohio and Kentucky where he had lived and worked, the John P. Parker legend persisted. Beverly Gray, a member of the Ohio Underground Railroad Association, who had been investigating sites for thirty years, was shocked one day when she visited a house in the middle of a Kentucky tobacco field not far from the Ohio River. The woman who owned the house was happy to give her a tour. When they reached a bedroom, the owner said matter-of-factly that this was the room from which "John Parker stole the baby."[1]

In the early 1990s, a high school principal in Ripley, Ohio, named

Hortense Parker Gilliam, John P. Parker's daughter, graduated from Mount Holyoke College in Massachusetts. All six of his children were college graduates.

Charles Nuckolls learned about John Parker's house. It was about to collapse, and Nuckolls tried to raise the money to save it. At about the same time, a Cincinnati civil rights lawyer named Robert Newman discovered the autobiography of John P. Parker while researching the life of the Reverend John Rankin in the Duke University archives. He learned of Nuckolls's attempts to save the Parker house and joined forces with him. Together, they founded the John P. Parker Historical Society. As for Parker's autobiography, Stuart Seely Sprague, a retired professor of history at Morehead State University in Kentucky, edited the manuscript and added information about Parker's life, and in 1996 the memoir was published by W.W. Norton & Co., ninety-six years after Parker's death. Proceeds from the sale of the book benefit the historical society.

The reissue of *Incidents in the Life of a Slave Girl, Written by Herself*, under the name of Harriet Jacobs in 1987 and the first publication of *His Promised Land: The Autobiography of John P. Parker, Former Slave and Conductor on the Underground Railroad* in 1996, came at the same time as a nationwide effort to rediscover the Underground Railroad. Over the years, the assumption grew that the Underground Railroad had been operated by whites, that Quakers and other white abolitionists had been the conductors and the stationmasters. The role played by blacks, both slave and free, in the Underground Railroad had barely been explored. Some presumed that blacks had played no role at all. Beginning in the 1980s, with the work of black historian Charles L. Blockson, attempts had been made to provide finally an accurate portrait of the tireless workers who ran the Underground Railroad. Blockson managed to trace his great-grandfather's escape to Canada. His cover story in the July 1984 issue of *National Geographic* is regarded by many as the beginning of the effort to preserve the remaining sites associated with the Underground Railroad and to document the people who were part of it, particularly the role blacks—including the slaves themselves—played in their escape.

In 1990, Congress authorized the National Park Service to conduct a study of the Underground Railroad, its routes, and operations in order to preserve and interpret this important chapter in U.S. history. A major part of the study was to identify the approximate routes taken by the slaves escaping to freedom. Another was to develop a set of exacting criteria for judging whether or not a site actually had been an Underground Railroad station, for over the course of almost 150 years many legends had arisen that could not necessarily be verified. As the writer of a January 2001 article on Underground Railroad sites in New York City put it, "Because stories of daring escapes and grass-roots collaboration are so compelling, there is a human desire to embrace them as true whatever their provenance. . . . While there are probably more trap doors than verifiable facts, there is much to honor." [2]

In 1998, President Bill Clinton signed into law the National Underground Railroad Network to Freedom Act. The money provided by the law will help fund the National Underground Railroad Freedom Center, an interactive learning facility. Located in Cincinnati, Ohio, it is scheduled to open in early 2004. Money authorized by Congress has also helped a number of states document their Underground Railroad history.

As with any attempt to preserve history, there have been exciting triumphs and aching failures. Government interest in and federal funding to preserve Underground Railroad sites probably saved the John P. Parker house in Ripley, Ohio. It definitely led to new investigations of places that had not been previously studied. As an example, the state of Maine now has several documented Underground Railroad sites, although sadly the urgency to document these locations was too late to save one of the most important.

The John Holyoke House was located in Brewer, Maine. Built in 1807, it sat high on a hill above the Penobscot River. John Holyoke, like many other influential citizens in Brewer and Bangor, believed that slavery was wrong and actively sought to abolish it. The area of the Penobscot River below his house was host to a wealth of ships and piers. Holyoke

President Bill Clinton signed the National Underground Railroad Network to Freedom Act in 1998.

had a tunnel built that led from the nearest pier to the basement of his house. Fugitive slaves who had made their way to Brewer could use that tunnel to reach Holyoke's house without being seen. The tunnel led to a hidden room in the basement, where the slaves stayed until they could be moved to an attic room in the house to hide. From there, they could continue their journey across a waterway route into Canada and freedom.

Local lore had long held that the house had been an Underground Railroad station. In the 1950s the owners of the house discovered the existence of the hidden room and began to suspect that it had been con-

Tunnels such as this were frequently used as hideouts and as passageways to keep fugitives out of sight.

nected to the shore by a tunnel. But they could not afford to do the major digging necessary to find out if the tunnel existed.

In the early 1990s, local authorities condemned the house and ordered it demolished to make way for a new bridge across the former waterway route to Canada. Historians and preservationists mounted a drive to save the beautiful old home, citing its architectural and historic importance. But no amount of public outcry could stave off the wrecker's ball. In 1995, the house was razed. During the demolition, in June 1995, a cotton shirt was found tucked into an eave next to one of the attic rooms. The shirt was hand stitched and simply constructed, with a drawstring collar and no buttons or other front closure. It was the type of shirt that would have been worn by a slave. The following year, the bulldozer being used to prepare the site uncovered the stone-lined tunnel.

The story is not unique. Very often in America we come to appreciate historical things only after we have lost them. But some good came out of the tragic loss of the John Holyoke House and the history it represented. A Maine Underground Railroad Association was established, and its members began to uncover other important stations in Maine.

In Brewer, Chamberlain Freedom Park was built, named for Joshua Chamberlain, who served as a Union general in the Civil War. Chamberlain grew up next door to the John Holyoke House. A bronze statue of Chamberlain was installed in the park, to be followed by a second bronze statue—this one of a slave.

Many states have created Freedom Trails, marking and tracing Underground Railroad routes and sites.

Notes

FOREWORD

1. Jacobs, Harriet A. *Incidents in the Life of a Slave Girl, Written by Herself*. Jean Fagan Yellin, ed. Cambridge, MA: Harvard University Press, 1987, p. 5.
2. Jacobs, *Incidents*, p. 6.
3. Parker, John P. *His Promised Land: The Autobiography of John P. Parker, Former Slave and Conductor on the Underground Railroad*. Stuart Seely Sprague, ed. New York: W.W. Norton and the John P. Parker Historical Society, 1996, p. 25.
4. Parker, *His Promised Land*, p. 27.
5. Parker, *His Promised Land*, p. 87.

CHAPTER 1. THE WILL TO BE FREE

1. Jacobs, *Incidents*, p. 28.
2. Parker, *His Promised Land*, p. 25.
3. Gerson, Evelyn. "Ona Judge Staines: A Thirst for Complete Freedom and Her Escape from President Washington." Master's thesis. World Wide Web version, copyright 2000 by Evelyn Gerson and SeacoastNH.com (www.seacoastnh.com/blackhistory/ona.html).
4. Gerson, "Ona Judge Staines," p. 3.
5. Gerson, "Ona Judge Staines," p. 5.
6. Gerson, "Ona Judge Staines," p. 7.
7. Parker, *His Promised Land*, p. 71.
8. "History of Tazewell County and the Underground Railroad," excerpted from *History of Tazewell Co., IL*. Chas. C. Chapman & Co., 1879, p. 313. World Wide Web version, copyright 1999-2000 by Candi Horton (www.iltrails.org/Tazewell/misc/undergro.htm).

CHAPTER 2. HARRIET JACOBS ESCAPES

1. Jacobs, *Incidents*, p. 97.
2. Jacobs, *Incidents*, Notes to XVII. "The Flight," n. 1, p. 274.
3. Jacobs, *Incidents*, Notes to XXVII. "New Destination for the Children," n. 3, p. 281.
4. Jacobs, *Incidents*, p. 161.

Sidebar—Following Freedom's Star
1. Jacqueline L. Tobin and Raymond G. Dobard, Ph.D., *Hidden in Plain View: A Secret Story of Quilts and the Underground Railroad*. New York: Anchor Books, 2000, p. 122.

CHAPTER 3. JOHN P. PARKER ESCAPES
1. Parker, *His Promised Land*, p. 30.
2. Parker, *His Promised Land*, p. 34.
3. Parker, *His Promised Land*, p. 54.
4. Parker, *His Promised Land*, p. 63.
5. Parker, *His Promised Land*, p. 70.

Sidebar—The Penalties for Aiding Fugitives: The Case of Delia Webster
1. http://www.nps.gov/boaf/site6.htm

Sidebar—Ozella Williams's Underground Railroad Quilt Code
1. Tobin and Dobard, *Hidden in Plain View*, p. 114.

CHAPTER 4. HARRIET JACOBS, FUGITIVE SLAVE IN THE NORTH
1. Jacobs, *Incidents*, p. 162.
2. Brown, William Wells. *Clotel, Or, The President's Daughter* (originally published 1853). New York: Modern Library, 2000, p. 32.
3. Jacobs, *Incidents*, p. 182.
4. Jacobs, *Incidents*, p.186.
5. Jacobs, *Incidents*, p. 200.

Sidebar—Slave Hunters
1. *Staats' Lockport City Directory for 1868–69*. Lockport: M.C. Richardson, 1868, p. 42.

Sidebar—The Fugitive Slave Act of 1850
1. Jacobs, *Incidents*, p. 191.

CHAPTER 5. JOHN P. PARKER, UNDERGROUND RAILROAD CONDUCTOR
1. Parker, *His Promised Land*, p. 93.
2. Parker, *His Promised Land*, p. 96.
3. Parker, *His Promised Land*, p. 103.
4. Parker, *His Promised Land*, p. 114.
5. Parker, *His Promised Land*, p. 144.

CHAPTER 6. THE GATHERING CLOUDS OF WAR
1. Jim Haskins, *Get on Board: The Story of the Underground Railroad*. New York: Scholastic, 1993, p. 126.
2. Haskins, *Get on Board*, p. 133.

CHAPTER 7. REDISCOVERING THE UNDERGROUND RAILROAD
1. Ann E. Eskridge and Sharon Fitzgerald. "There's a Movement Afoot: The Underground Railroad." *American Visions*, February/March 1999, p. 40.
2. Sandee Brawarsky, "Safe Havens on the Freedom Line." *The New York Times*, January 19, 2001, p. 46.

Bibliography

BOOKS

Brown, William Wells. *Clotel, Or; The President's Daughter* (originally published 1853). New York: Modern Library, 2000.

Haskins, Jim. *Get on Board: The Story of the Underground Railroad*. New York: Scholastic, 1993.

Jacobs, Harriet A. *Incidents in the Life of a Slave Girl, Written by Herself*. Jean Fagan Yellin, ed. Cambridge, MA: Harvard University Press, 1987.

Parker, John P. *His Promised Land: The Autobiography of John P. Parker, Former Slave and Conductor on the Underground Railroad*. Stuart Seely Sprague, ed. New York: W.W. Norton and the John P. Parker Historical Society, 1996.

Staats' Lockport City Directory for 1868–69. Lockport: M.C. Richardson, 1868.

Tobin, Jacqueline L., and Raymond G. Dobard. *Hidden in Plain View: A Secret Story of Quilts and the Underground Railroad*. New York: Anchor Books, 2000.

ARTICLES

Brawarsky, Sandee. "Safe Havens on the Freedom Line." *The New York Times*, January 19, 2001, p. E37+.

Curtis, John Obed. "Following the Drinking Gourd." *Early American Homes*, vol. 29, no. 1, February 1998, pp. 34–36.

Eskridge, Ann E., and Sharon Fitzgerald. "There's a Movement Afoot: The Underground Railroad." *American Visions*, February/March 1999, pp. 40–46.

Jacobs, John S. "A True Tale of Slavery." *Leisure Hour* (London), vol. 10 (1861), pp. 85–86.

Jones, Katherine Butler. "They Called It Timbucto." *Orion*, vol. 17, no. 1, Winter 1998, pp. 27–33.

Price, H.H. "History Happened Here: The Story of the Underground Railroad in Maine." *Legacy*, September/October 1997, pp. 20–25.

WEBSITE

National Underground Railroad Freedom Center website: www.undergroundrailroad.org.

Further Reading

Bentley, Judith. *Dear Friend: Thomas Garrett & William Still, Collaborators on the Underground Railroad*. New York: Cobblehill Books, 1997.

Brill, Marlene Targ. *Allen Jay and the Underground Railroad*. Minneapolis, MN: Carolrhoda Books, 1993.

Gorrell, Gena K. *North Star to Freedom: The Story of the Underground Railroad*. New York: Delacorte Press, 1997.

Greenwood, Barbara. *The Last Safe House: A Story of the Underground Railroad*. Toronto: Kids Can Press, 1998.

Haskins, Jim. *The Day Fort Sumter Was Fired On*. New York: Scholastic, 1995.

Hopkinson, Deborah. *Sweet Clara and the Freedom Quilt*. New York: Knopf, 1993.

Levine, Ellen. *If You Traveled on the Underground Railroad*. New York: Scholastic, 1992.

Index

Page numbers for illustrations are in **boldface**.

111